BONHOEFFER

BONHOEFFER
Prophet and Martyr

John Henry Queripel

RESOURCE *Publications* • Eugene, Oregon

BONHOEFFER
Prophet and Martyr

Copyright © 2016 John Henry Queripel. All rights reserved. Except for brief quotations in critical publications or reviews, no part of this book may be reproduced in any manner without prior written permission from the publisher. Write: Permissions, Wipf and Stock Publishers, 199 W. 8th Ave., Suite 3, Eugene, OR 97401.

Resource Publications
An Imprint of Wipf and Stock Publishers
199 W. 8th Ave., Suite 3
Eugene, OR 97401

www.wipfandstock.com

PAPERBACK ISBN 13: 978-1-4982-2960-9
HARDCOVER ISBN 13: 978-1-4982-2962-3

Manufactured in the U.S.A.   01/12/2016

Contents

Dietrich Bonhoeffer—A Life of Witness | 1

Bonhoeffer—Prophet and Martyr
A play by John Queripel | 35

    List of Characters | 37
    Act 1 | 39
    Act 2 | 43
    Act 3 | 60
    Act 4 | 74
    Act 5 | 82
    Act 6 | 99
    Act 7 | 105

DIETRICH BONHOEFFER
A Life of Witness

The circuitous route taken by Dietrich Bonhoeffer's captors in the dying days of the Third Reich to his place of execution, from the Gestapo Prinz-Albrecht-Strasse prison in Berlin, to Buchenwald, Flossenburg, Regensburg, Schonberg, and finally back to Flossenburg, was in stark clear contrast to the single-minded clear certainty with which Dietrich Bonhoeffer moved toward his death. On arrival finally at that place, Flossenburg—forever associated with him, though he spent only some twelve hours there—Bonhoeffer was given a summary trial, court martialled on the evening of his arrival, before being crudely executed the following morning, April 9, 1945, only weeks from the war's end with the guns of the Allies sounding in the distance. Three weeks later, Adolf Hitler, the one who had ordered Bonhoeffer's execution, was dead by his own hand. A week after that suicide the "thousand-year Reich" was no more.

Why would Hitler have concerned himself with the execution of a Lutheran pastor and why would a pastor be facing a court martial? The answer to those questions is that this pastor was indeed one who was very different. Originally drawn to the idea of non-violent resistance as typified by Mahatma Gandhi, whom he so wished to visit, Dietrich Bonhoeffer had ended up part of military intelligence, the Abwehr, and was even deeply involved in their plot to kill Hitler. The best known of these failed plots, that of July 20, 1944, linked with Colonel Claus von Stauffenberg, was the reason why the tyrannical ruler, even in what he should have known to be the final weeks of his rule, found it necessary in an act of vengeance to personally order the execution of all those involved in plots to overthrow the regime. Thus, on that morning Bonhoeffer died in the company of General Wilhelm Canaris, under whose command he had been at the Abwehr, and other conspirators including Major General Hans Oster and Judge Advocate Karl Sack.

Dietrich Bonhoeffer was not the only one of his family involved in the conspiratorial plots to kill Hitler. Far from it! Indeed the whole family was involved in opposition to the Nazis with a number actively joining the conspiracy, and for that the family would pay dearly. In martyrdom Dietrich was joined by his brother Klaus and two of his brother-in-laws, Hans von Dohnanyi, who had recruited him to the Abwehr, and Rudiger Schleicher. Given the chaos of the final weeks of the war and those days following immediately after, it was to be a couple of months after his execution that both the parents and also the fiancée of Dietrich Bonhoeffer were to have their worst fears cruelly confirmed. That the parents had Bonhoeffer's death confirmed from listening to a radio broadcast of a memorial service being held for him in London shows the great esteem in which Dietrich Bonhoeffer was already being held. Of course that estimation has continued to grow over the succeeding years.

That esteem in which Bonhoeffer is held is not only due to his brave martyrdom but also for his brilliant theological mind, and it could fairly be said that much of modern theological thought finds its roots in this man's writings. Given that he was only thirty-nine when he was executed, one is only left to ponder what brilliant subsequent thought was consigned to the grave with him. The preliminary thoughts of future works he was considering, smuggled from prison, give some indication but also teasingly leave much to conjecture. A couple of those letters in particular addressed to his great friend Eberhard Bethge, in which he spoke of 'religionless Christianity,' has led to all sorts of speculation as to where Bonhoeffer's thoughts were going.

Dietrich Bonhoeffer—A Life of Witness

Dietrich Bonhoeffer was born into a prominent German family with both sides of the family being well connected. His father, Karl Bonhoeffer, a leading psychiatrist, held the foremost chair in the field in Germany at the Berlin University from his appointment in 1912 until his death in 1948, and ironically in that role he would be pressed into service in examining Marius van der Lubbe, the Dutch Communist almost certainly framed by the Nazis, for starting the Reichstag (German Parliament) fire. Bonhoeffer's mother, Paula von Hase, a teacher, was likewise from a prominent family. Her parents been connected to the emperor's court at Potsdam, while her grandfather Karl had been a famous theologian and both her father and brother were pastors. It could be argued that the deep religious conviction of Dietrich Bonhoeffer found its genesis on the maternal side of the family while his rigorous questioning found its roots in the more religiously sceptical paternal side of the family. The Bonhoeffer family thus were very much part of the cultural and intellectual elite in Germany, and from such circles, often shocked by the common vulgar brutality of the Nazis, would come much of the opposition to Hitler.

The young Dietrich was intellectually precocious, his reflections made on a trip to Rome when just eighteen on the links between the culture of antiquity of the classical world and that of modern Europe bearing strong witness to that. During that same trip to Italy Bonhoeffer began also to reflect upon the nature of the church, with his narrow nationalist understanding of the church, a view shared by almost all Germans of the time, being challenged by the universal nature of the Roman Church with its huge range of cultures present in the Vatican. This experience largely led to Bonhoeffer's doctorate, "Sanctorum Communio: A Dogmatic Inquiry into the Sociology of the Church," along with his post-doctorate, *Act and Being*. In contrast to the narrow nationalism of the German church, Bonhoeffer's wider universal view would make him less susceptible later to the propaganda of the Nazis, who, drawing from Luther, equated the Christian message and German nationalism and thus were able to draw the great majority of the German church to their cause.

Bonhoeffer's doctorate was completed within the highly prestigious theological faculty of the University of Berlin by the time he was just twenty-one. That faculty had as its iconic figure the father of modern liberal Christian thought, Friedrich Schleiermacher (1768–1834), and still heavily bore his influence. During the time of Bonhoeffer's studies the faculty head was another paradigmatic figure within liberal Christian thought, Adolf von Harnack (1851–1930). While the liberal views of the faculty may have been met with familial understanding, though much of the family thought Dietrich's brilliance was wasted in theology, they left Bonhoeffer unsatisfied. While not opposed to Christianity the Bonhoeffer family, as typified by his father Karl, had imbibed deeply from a more empirical scientific source. As Professor of Psychiatry Karl Bonhoeffer was an empiricist with little time for the emerging psychoanalytical movement led by such figures as Sigmund Freud, Carl Jung, and Alfred Adler. Family discussions were set by a need to be concise and to have clarity in thinking, with overdone appeals to emotion frowned upon. This environment set the course for the Bonhoeffer siblings, with Dietrich's brother Klaus choosing a career in law, rising in that profession to be the top lawyer for the German airline Lufthansa, and Karl Friedrich distinguishing himself as a brilliant physicist working with such figures as Albert Einstein and Max Planck in the quest to split the atom. The Bonhoeffer family were not churchgoers, although Paula as mother along with her familial church background had been imbued with the piety of the "Herrnhut movement" and so ensured that regular Bible reading and hymn singing were a part of the family life.

Though Dietrich Bonhoeffer's theological training took place in an institution synonymous with the German historical-critical method, that was not to be the system of thought which most influenced him. Instead his major influence came from a man who stood irrevocably opposed to that liberal tradition, the Swiss theologian Karl Barth (1886–1968), who had shaken the theological world when in 1922, while working as a rural pastor, he wrote a commentary on Romans that represented the beginning of his sustained attack on theological liberalism. Theological liberalism had equated European progress, thought, and culture with Christian theology, stating that the gospel must be couched in such a manner to make sense in that context. Of course when Barth wrote Europe had just passed through the catastrophic war of 1914–18, making such an easy accommodation of the gospel to European culture much more problematic. In response Barth developed a system of theological thought resolutely opposed to all for which the liberal tradition stood. The liberal system, its father being Schleiermacher, had been the norm in the European theological tradition for over a century and of course much of it was centred on Bonhoeffer's alma mater, the theological faculty within the University of Berlin. So entrenched was theological liberalism that the contribution of Barth represented 'a bolt out of the blue.' While the liberal project had seen culture and faith as analogous, believing the task of theology to be to speak coherently and sensibly to the culture, Barth charged that faith instead stood dialectically rather than analogously to culture and far from acting as the affirmation of culture stood instead dialectically as its great "no." Human beings from within their framework of culture and tradition were totally unable to work their way to God, who always stood above and outside the human project looking down from a height on the human towers of Babel. Barth's God was utterly transcendent and there were no means by which humans could win divine approval through their own methods, but rather salvation could only come from the divine side mediated as grace through Jesus Christ. As such it cast a great judgement upon all human effort.

Barth understood his theology as a restatement of the Protestant orthodoxy of "sola fides," that one could only be saved through faith. That in particular had been the experience of the founder of Protestantism, Martin Luther, a man whose figure towered over Germany. However, though Protestantism in essence rejected any idea that one could achieve salvation through their own means or through participation in a particular culture, the historical reality that Protestantism had been founded in Germany by a German, Luther, and represented a break with the universal church meant that the Protestant faith had ironically become deeply linked with what it meant to be German, so that the two had almost become synonymous. Martin Luther, who had stood against the universal church, was viewed as a German hero and in his opposition to the universal nature of the Catholic Church was understood to be the one in which German particular identity was created and centred. By his translation of the Latin Vulgate into German Luther had also largely codified a language unifying the disparate Germanic traditions into a greater sense of oneness, though that process of unity would not culminate until Bismarck established the German nation in 1871. Given this context, the Protestant church and in particular the Lutheran church had strongly developed as a German nationalist church.

The Lutheran church also importantly had a very particular way of understanding faith in relation to the political order. The theological centre point of the Lutheran faith, as we have just seen, was that a person is entirely dependent on the grace of God for salvation, with no one being able to save themselves. This thought of course had a radical outworking within the political and social order by stripping away all distinctions of self-righteousness and in so doing had a revolutionary impact in that it undermined a class system at that time firmly set within the framework of feudalism. If no one was more justified than anyone else before the great Lord then why should one seek justification before the lesser lords? Rather, each person was equal before the magisterial divine. Understanding the political implications of this theological thought, the German peasants began a rebellion against that old order they no longer viewed as having divine sanction. Initially Luther was supportive of the peasants, but then turned against them in the style of vile language that perhaps only Luther could muster, urging the princes to "smite slay and stab" the peasants, before adding, "such wonderful times are these that a prince can merit heaven better with bloodshed than another with prayer."[1]

The sudden turn of Luther's sympathies is best explained of course

---

1. "Against the Robbing and Murdering Hordes of Peasants," May 1525, quoted in Harold J. Grimm, *The Reformation Era, 1500–1650*, 2nd ed. (New York: Macmillan, 1973) 143.

by his realisation that he needed the support of the German princes if his Reformation was to succeed in face of the power of the Holy Roman Empire. What seemed to be a logical nexus between the theological idea that all people, in total need of grace, were equal before God with the sociopolitical outworking that therefore no one should be privileged and that all were equal, had to be broken. Luther did this by separating the religious and the secular realm. In the former, yes, all were equal in that all were equally dependent on God's grace, but this was to be held entirely separate from the political realm in which the old order would prevail. Lutheran thought would operate by a stark dualism whereby the religious and secular realms were held separate. The church was to only be concerned with the realm of faith but must remain mute in the secular realm which properly belonged to the state for state authorities like those in the church had been placed in those positions by the Divine will. They drew especially from the Scripture passage "for there is no authority except from God, and those that exist have been instituted by God" (Rom 13:1) for this view, along with the passage calling one to "render Caesar that which belongs to Caesar and unto God that which belongs to God" (Mark 12:17).

This dualist understanding was to strongly shape the German church response to the Nazis, largely precluding the church from mounting an effective opposition to that regime. That response to the regime, however, did vary.

I response of a large part of the church was that represented by the German Christians, those who completely fell in behind the Nazi Reich not only understanding it as being like other political leadership as being established by God, but going further by seeing the Nazis as having a special providential role. Led by such figures as Ludwig Muller, later made Reichsbishop of the Reichskirche (the unified German Protestant Church) by the Nazis, the German Christians offered total support to the regime, gladly superimposing the swastika with the cross. Selling themselves completely to the Nazis, they viewed Hitler and the Nazis as saviours divinely sent in order to save Germany from both the ignominy of the strictures placed on the nation by the Treaty of Versailles and also from the Communist threat both from within and outside Germany. They identified the Weimar Republic with German weakness, both of which had been a result of Versailles, and its weakness they understood as fuelling the atheistic Communist threat. Further, they joined the Nazis in seeing the Jews as the integral part of an international "Zionist conspiracy" being behind the Weimar Republic, and viewed both the Jews and that Republic as being part of a planned "Zionist-Communist" takeover. The Jews were understood in this to be a fifth column, a traitorous festering sore within Germany. In order to create this narrative, Jesus of course had to be rebirthed as a classic Aryan hero who had been betrayed and executed by this perfidious race. In one sense, however, the German Christians were not classically Lutheran, for they were all too eager to hand over control of the church, the properly religious realm, to the Nazis. The German Christians came later to dominate the Reichskirche and the same could be said also of that body.

The main alternative response to that of both the German Christians and the Reichskirche was that initially represented by the Pastors' Emergency League and then later the Confessing Church. The response of both these fell classically within the duality of the Lutheran framework, in that they largely ceded the political sphere to the Nazis but strongly opposed Nazi interference in the religious realm. Opposing the Reichskirche for their selling out of the properly religious sphere to the Nazis, the Confessing Church, because of their dualist understandings, were never able to offer the needed strength of opposition to the regime. While unable to offer the needed resistance to the Nazis, from within their dualist framework they were able to arrive however at a point where they separated themselves from the Reichskirche and viewed it as having lost the right to call itself church by its surrender of the realm that was properly religious by allowing its doctrine to be infected with the regime's ideology. The Barmen Declaration of 1934, largely written by Karl Barth, is the best known document representing the Confessing Church framework and as the foundation document of the Confessing Church it centres not on a critique of Nazi policy in general but rather on the defence only of the properly religious realm from attack by the Nazis. For not opposing this, the Confessing Church through this declaration charged that the Reichskirche no longer had the right to be called church, for by taking on "alien principles" it "ceases to be the church." The declaration rejected the idea that the church should shape its message to "the prevailing ideological and political convictions," for no part of the church's life can belong "to other Lords." It further stated, "We reject as the false doctrine, as though the state over and beyond its special commission should and could become the single and totalitarian order of human life, thus fulfilling the church's vocation as well."

A clear example of the Confessing Church's dualist and therefore limited opposition to the Nazis was the view they held concerning Nazi policies toward the Jews. Numerous Jews and Jewish families in Germany over the centuries had converted to Christianity and were part of the church, with Dietrich Bonhoeffer's close friend Franz Hildebrandt being one such person, having even become a pastor in the Lutheran Church. Bonhoeffer's twin sister, Sabine, had even married such a person, Gerhard Liebholz. Bonhoeffer assisted all of them in their later escape from Germany, but one episode he deeply regretted in which he felt he had failed the Liebholz family was when under pressure from his district superintendent Bonhoeffer refused to preach at the funeral of Gerhard's father due to his being Jewish and not being baptised as a Christian. This memory particularly haunted Bonhoeffer.

The Nazis of course viewed being Jewish not as a religious belief held concerning Judaism but rather as a gene contained within, i.e., racially, whatever one's belief. Thus for them all those of Jewish background in the church were still Jews and Jews were being increasingly persecuted in Germany. Caught in its dualist understanding, the Confessing Church mounted a defence for those Jews within the church but was never able to rise in defence of those outside it. Bonhoeffer, although he had been among the founders of both the Pastors' Emergency League and the Confessing Church, finally felt that the limits of its response to the increasing terror felt by the Jews at the hands of the Nazis was too narrowly premised, and his famous cry became, "only those who cry out for the Jews may also sing Gregorian chants."[2] Bonhoeffer had now moved from his early response to the regime, seen in his initial radio address two days after the Nazis had come to power in January 1933, where he critiqued the ideology of the leader (German literally "fuhrer") when it claimed too much for itself thereby becoming idolatrous and taking the place of the one to whom praise ought be offered thereby, to a point where he was among very few in the church prepared to oppose the Nazis ethically and politically as well as for their religious policies. Bonhoeffer's opposition was best expressed by his well known words, we "are not just to bandage the victims under the wheel, but to put a spoke in the wheel itself."[3] For Bonhoeffer it was clearly necessary to stop the state carrying out evil not just in the religious realm but wherever and against whomever it was being perpetrated. Such thinking led to Bonhoeffer's later involvement in the conspiracy and even to be part of the plot to assassinate the Fuhrer. The journey to such a position must not of course have been easy for one who had at one stage been so drawn to the non-violent resistance of Gandhi.

Not only did the church have difficulty opposing the Nazi regime, but the military did also. Deeply imbued by a culture of obedience to the state as legitimate authority, opposition to the regime represented a massive step for those within the military who chose to make it. That disobedience to the regime had been made even more difficult by the Nazis, who had made the military pledge an oath of obedience to Adolf Hitler as their Fuhrer. Such oaths were seriously regarded in military circles. Despite this the plots against Hitler were centred within the military, particularly in its high circles, and it is among this circle Bonhoeffer found himself as a member of military intelligence, the Abwehr. Many within those ranks of the military gave their lives for that involvement.

2. James W. Woelfel, *Bonhoeffer's Theology: Classical and Revolutionary* (Nashville: Abingdon, 1970) 248.

3. Dietrich Bonhoeffer, *No Rusty Swords: Letters, Lectures and Notes, 1928–1936*, edited by Edwin H. Robertson, translated by Edwin H. Robertson (London: Collins, 1970) 221.

To return to the German church and the heritage it inherited from Martin Luther, one cannot of course pass without considering the church's attitude to the Jews. Luther originally had been very understanding of the Jews and why they had not converted to Christianity, speaking of their non-conversion as a result of Christians acting as "beasts" toward them. He even wrote as essay on how Jesus Christ had been born a Jew. Towards the end of his life, however, he became more and more the "grumpy old man," lambasting pretty much everything and everyone in ever more vulgar language, and that included becoming an extreme anti-Semite. Thus he advocated in his essay "On the Jews and Their Lies" setting fire to Jewish synagogues and schools, destroying homes, confiscating of Jewish prayer books, expropriating their money, and putting them to work in forced labour. The Nazis of course were to gleefully make great use of such material from the German hero, but not only the Nazis but the Protestant church attitude in general to the Jews also had been long tainted by such words from its founder. The anti-Semitism of the Nazis did not arise out of barren ground but had a long history of being planted in fertile soil.

The sort of issues with which Bonhoeffer was involved increasingly sharpened of course his theological analysis. That contextual sharpness is initially seen in his *Cost of Discipleship*, published November 1937. In that work Bonhoeffer contrasted "cheap grace" with "costly grace." God's grace, he noted, had been too easily given by the church to the whole German community with the result that it had lost any real meaning. We have baptised a nation, Bonhoeffer charged, with a cheap grace that made no demands to live in discipleship as Christians. Rather, grace was free but never cheap, as God's giving of grace was centred in the cross of Jesus and was therefore a most costly grace. Cheap grace had only served to provide justification for whatever was carried out in the name of Christ, and made no demand for lives to be Christlike. Instead of being a recipient of cheap grace, the Christian is called to costly discipleship. "When Christ calls a person, he bids them come and die," cried Bonhoeffer, and "only the one who believes is obedient, and only the one who is obedient believes,"[4] thereby challenging the shallow and complacent religiosity passing itself as faith.

Bonhoeffer's next major work, never actually completed, was *Ethics*. Clearly, in his increasing involvement in the conspiracy Bonhoeffer was moving in places where Christian ethics had little if anything to say. In this work Bonhoeffer called the Christian to go past absolute ethical ideas, which all too often serve as a means of opting out of decision making and action. Rather than maintaining moral purity by adhering to an abstract ideal, a Kantian ethical imperative, a Christian is called to action in obedience to the call and will of God. Too often, he wrote, Christians were reduced to inaction due to their often ego-centred concern for their moral purity rather than getting actively involved in a world where ethical decisions were not usually black or white and involved acting in a manner contrary to absolutes. Truth of itself, he noted, had no absolute value as a moral imperative. In order to show such, Bonhoeffer posed the example of a child asked at school in front of the class as to whether his father was a drunkard. In such circumstances Bonhoeffer charged there was no obligation to tell the truth. Equally, Bonhoeffer in his conspiratorial role in the Abwehr felt no obligation to tell the truth but rather to the Nazis would live a life of deception. What was of prime importance to him was devotion to God and the living out God's will, and this trumped all moral and ethical imperatives. Thus Bonhoeffer felt himself increasingly called to such action even if that sullied his own moral conscience. He even spoke of how if his actions condemned him to eternal torment he must accept this, for such actions, even at the expense of one's soul, were the disciple's call and duty. With their own ethical questions, many in the conspiracy looked to Bonhoeffer for guidance as to their duty, and that adherence to duty was to eventually cost many in the conspiracy, including of course Bonhoeffer, their own lives.

4. Dietrich Bonhoeffer, *The Cost of Discipleship*, translated by R. H. Fuller (New York: Macmillan, 1979) 99, 69.

It was while he was imprisoned in Tegel that Bonhoeffer wrote a series of theological reflections, which for the most part were smuggled out of the prison. These became the basis for the third major writing associated with Dietrich Bonhoeffer, his *Letters and Papers from Prison*. As earlier said, the thoughts expressed in these are especially tantalising, as clearly most of them are only worked out in a nascent preliminary form, Bonhoeffer's intention being to further expand on them after his release from prison. That release of course never came.

The teasing kernel of the work comes in letter dated April 30, 1944. It is good to quote it extensively because even as it is in full it is clearly but a précis of where Bonhoeffer's thought was taking him. He begins by expressing his hope for the success of one of the upcoming plans to assassinate Hitler. "I think," he writes, "God is about to accomplish something that, even if we take part in it either outwardly or inwardly, we can only receive with the greatest awe." He follows then with some theological reflections in which he clearly understands himself as broaching new ground. "What is bothering me incessantly," he writes,

> is the question what Christianity really is, for us today. The time when people could be told everything by means of words, whether theological or pious, is over, and so is the time of inwardness and conscience—and that means the time of religion in general. We are moving towards a completely religionless time. . . . Our whole nineteen-hundred-year-old preaching and theology rest on the "religious a priori" of humankind. "Christianity" has always been a form—perhaps the true form—of "religion." But if one day it becomes clear that this a priori does not exist at all, but was a historically conditioned and transient form of human self-expression, and if therefore humans become radically religionless—and I think that that is already more or less the case . . . what does that mean for "Christianity"? It means that the foundation

is taken away from the whole of what to now been our "Christianity."[5]

It could be argued that this style of thought stands within the Barthian neo-orthodox tradition which had so shaped Bonhoeffer, but Bonhoeffer as I understand is clearly carrying Barth's conclusions further:

> Barth, who is the only one to have started along this line of thought, did not carry it to completion, but arrived at a positivism of revelation, which in the last analysis is essentially a restoration. For the religionless working person (or any other person) nothing decisive is gained here. The questions to be answered would surely be: What do a church, a community, a sermon, a liturgy, a Christian life mean in a religionless world? How do we speak of God—without religion? . . . How do we speak (or perhaps we cannot now speak as we used to) in a "secular" way about "God"? In what way are we "religionless-secular" Christians, in what way are we the "ek-klesia" [*NB: Greek literally 'called out,' from which we get our word ecclesial*], those who are called forth, not regarding ourselves from a religious point of view as specially favoured, but rather as belonging wholly to the world?[6]

Again just four days before the von Stauffenberg plot, July 16, 1944, Bonhoeffer wrote,

> The God who is with us is the God who forsakes us (Mark 15:34). The God who lets us live in the world without the working hypothesis of God is the God before whom we stand continually. Before God and with God we live without God. God lets himself be pushed out of the world onto the cross. He is weak and powerless in the world, and that is precisely the way, the only way, in which he is with us and helps us.[7]

---

5. Dietrich Bonhoeffer, *Letters and Papers from Prison*, edited by Eberhard Bethge, rev. ed. (New York: Macmillan, 1971) 279–80.

6. Ibid., 280–81.

7. Ibid., 360.

The day following the unsuccessful von Stauffenberg plot, Bonhoeffer wrote,

> During the last year or so I've come to know and understand more and more the profound this-worldliness of Christianity. The Christian is not a homo-religiosus, but simply a person, as Jesus was a man—in contrast, shall we say to John the Baptist. . . . By this-worldliness I mean living unreservedly in life's duties, problems, successes and failures, experiences and perplexities.[8]

Clearly Bonhoeffer writing in such manner is an expression of his interests and actions having moved far beyond the sphere of religion to the down-to-earth questions of living in the midst of the ambiguity of the world. Of course his thinking in such secular manner had been strongly shaped by his ongoing involvement in the conspiracy that he was hoping as he wrote was about to culminate successfully in the most extensive and best known of the plots on Hitler's life.

This tantalising reflection of Bonhoeffer's thought has led to much speculation as to where Bonhoeffer may have taken the theological world if he had survived the war. As earlier stated, I believe that Bonhoeffer was past a mere restatement of Barthian neo-orthodoxy, though holding to its essential anti-religiosity. It is clear from his words above that he has left behind a view that merely replaced a "via-positiva," working from the world to God, with a "via-negativa" and therefore a need for revelation from God, for such revelation leaves us still in the religious realm and is therefore irrelevant in the radically secular world of which Bonhoeffer speaks. Bonhoeffer's view of the secularity of the world and therefore the absence of God as a premise needed to make sense of existence, led in the 1960s to the "death of God" school of theologians including Harvey Cox, Bishop John Robinson, and Thomas Altizer, while his call for action in the pained reality of the world found voice in the liberation theologians primarily associated with

8. Ibid., 369–70.

South America, figures such as Gustavo Gutierrez, Lenonardo Boff, and Juan Segundo.

Bonhoeffer also presented an ecclesiastical challenge to the church, writing in his April 30, 1944 letter of the church in a secular age being made up of

> a few intellectually dishonest people, on whom we can descend as "religious." Are these to be the chosen few? Is it on this dubious group of people that we are to pounce in fervour, pique or indignation, in order to sell them our goods? Are we to fall upon a few unfortunate people in their hour of need and exercise a sort of religious compulsion upon them? If we don't want to do all that, if our final judgement must be that the western form of Christianity, too, was only a preliminary stage to a complete absence of religion, what kind of situation emerges for us in the church? How can Christ become the Lord of the religionless as well? Are there religionless Christians?[9]

Clearly again in his ecclesial understanding Bonhoeffer was visualising a future—perhaps already then becoming present—in which seemingly the religious domain, along with its vehicle, the church, was redundant.

While in the Tegel prison Bonhoeffer clearly hoped to be released, and that real hope remained present for him right up the failure of the von Stauffenberg plot and the subsequent discovery of the Zossen files. Bonhoeffer was treated well at Tegel, almost certainly due to his uncle on his mother's side being General Paul von Hase, the military commandant of Berlin and therefore in charge ultimately of the military prison. Bonhoeffer, however, never took advantage of this fortuitous relationship, sharing with other prisoners the goods sent to him by his family and refusing on one occasion the offer of moving to a better cell, though at one point Bonhoeffer was visited by his uncle armed with plenty of sekt (German champagne), which they shared together with a few others. Paul von Hase was also involved in the conspiratorial

---

9. Ibid., 280.

movement, an involvement that would cost him his life just six weeks after that visit to Bonhoeffer.

Bonhoeffer had a particular reason for wanting to be released from the Tegel prison: his engagement with Maria von Wedemeyer, only concluded a matter of months before his arrest. This action alone represented a change in Bonhoeffer's theological understanding. Previous to this he had a relationship with a fellow theological student, Elizabeth Zinn, and this lasted eight years before Bonhoeffer increasingly distanced himself from the relationship, believing that, given the context in which he found himself, there were seemingly more important things to do. Now, however, with Maria his attitude had changed to one in which deeply human, life-affirming things such as love must be celebrated. It was almost as though he was saying, "What greater protest against a surrounding nihilist culture of death, seemingly closing off from any future, could there be than the concluding of a marriage celebrating love and a commitment to the future?"

Maria was the granddaughter of a dear friend, Ruth von Kleist-Retzow, who had long been a supporter of Dietrich Bonhoeffer from the time he had been directing the Confessing Church seminaries and collective pastorates in Pomerania, eastern Germany, where she lived on a country estate. Bonhoeffer had seen Maria grow, from a child he considered too young to join the confirmation classes he conducted for her older siblings, into a young woman. It seems that he became increasingly attracted to her until he became smitten with her in May 1942—feelings about which she had no idea at that stage and which she did not share for him. She was only eighteen, after all, while he was an eminent figure aged thirty-six.

It was not until three months later, August 1942, that Bonhoeffer was able to return to the estate, having had no contact with her over that period. While he was there tragic news came that Ruth's son Hans, Maria's father, had been killed at Stalingrad, aged fifty-four. Not long after Maria's older brother, Max, who had been part of the family confirmation class conducted by Bonhoeffer, was also killed. Possibly through Bonhoeffer's pastoral care and sensitivity at the time, he and Maria grew closer, prompted by Ruth the grandmother, but resisted by Maria's mother Ruth, who forbade Bonhoeffer to come to her son's funeral. Eventually Maria's mother relented and agreed to the relationship on the stringent grounds that there be a year separation and restricted correspondence. In ordinary times those conditions would have been onerous enough, but in the place in which Dietrich Bonhoeffer found himself it was like an eternity. He eventually proposed to her by letter January 10, 1943.

Less than three months later he would be arrested. Visits subsequent to that, while Bonhoeffer was held at Tegel, would be made under the watchful eye of Judge Advocate Manfred Roeder. During those visits both spoke enthusiastically of their wedding plans and even set a date for the celebration, for both were certain that Bonhoeffer's incarceration would only be temporary. As time went on, however, with Bonhoeffer still in prison Maria fell deeper and deeper into despair. The wedding of course never took place, and after Bonhoeffer was transferred to the Gestapo's Prinz-Albrecht-Strasse prison they never saw each other again. Following the war's end with the defeat of the Nazis, Maria sought out every lead as to where Bonhoeffer might be, and like Dietrich's parents she would only find out his fate months after his execution had been carried out. It is not as though Bonhoeffer had no choice concerning that future which led to his arrest and execution. He had numerous opportunities to choose an easier and more amenable path, but instead Bonhoeffer resolutely set his face to where he knew his actions would most likely take him, and in that walk he was unflinching. He could have remained a part of the Confessing Church opposition and saved his own life at the expense, no doubt, given his prominent position, of time in prison, like Martin Niemoller, who spent twelve years incarcerated by the Nazis, only being released by the Allies at the war's end.

Faced with a crisis decision early in 1939 when all men born in his year were called up for military service, Bonhoeffer even had the opportunity to have the safety of the Atlantic between him and the Nazis. Of course Bonhoeffer had no desire to fight for the

Nazis, but there was no option of conscientious objection as such people were simply shot. He could, however, defer his service, and he did that by taking up an offer made through his ecumenical contacts to travel to the safety of the United States, accepting an offer of two roles there that would enable him to ride out the war in safety. There his prominent supporters, among them Reinhold Niebuhr, had secured him a teaching position at arguably the nation's leading theological seminary, Union, in New York, along with another offer at the "Central Bureau for Interchurch Aid." Bonhoeffer, however, soon after having committed to this course, began to have doubts as to his path, those doubts coming as early as his voyage to the U.S. By the time of his arrival he was intensely conflicted and could find no peace in this sanctuary, instead being increasingly convinced that he must return to Germany. Writing to Niebuhr he noted, "I shall have no right, to participate in the reconstruction of Christian life in Germany after the war if I do not share the trials of this time with my people." Finally he announced on June 20, 1939 that he would not take up the positions offered him, but instead would return to a Germany set for war. That war broke out just five weeks after his return.

Another opportunity to escape his end came during his time in Tegel. Dietrich Bonhoeffer was well regarded by both the guards and other prisoners, with many of the former helping him smuggle out numerous letters, many of which became his *Letters and Papers from Prison*. With those letters not having to pass the censor's eye, Bonhoeffer could be more open about his circumstances and also pass on and receive news about the political situation, in particular plans having to do with the conspiracy. One of the guards with whom Bonhoeffer became particularly friendly was Corporal Knoblauch. With the assistance of the corporal Bonhoeffer was planning his escape around the time the Zossen files were found. The plan was simply for Bonhoeffer to walk out of the prison dressed as a mechanic, and to that end the Bonhoeffer family had delivered the requisite clothes to Knoblauch. However, when the Gestapo arrested his brother Klaus, Bonhoeffer gave up the plan as it would direct more suspicion upon his brother and to others with whom he was linked in the Abwehr circle. It was not long after that that Bonhoeffer, following the discovery of the Zossen files on September 20, 1944, was transferred to the Gestapo prison at Prinz-Albrecht-Strasse on October 8, 1944. The fallout from the discovery of the Zossen files saw many of his fellow conspirators, including Carl Goerdeler, (the Mayor of Leipzig) Fr. Joseph Muller, army Judge Advocate General Karl Sack, and First Lieutenant Fabian von Schladrendorff, join him there. Only the last named would not share the same end as Bonhoeffer, instead having a miraculous reprieve as we shall see. As for Knoblauch, nothing is known of what transpired after the war.

Dietrich Bonhoeffer had yet another opportunity to escape his end in the dying days of the war immediately prior to his execution. As part of that disparate group being taken south from Buchenwald as the allies closed in, the British intelligence agent Captain S. Payne Best encouraged the group to seek their liberty, for clearly those guarding them already had one eye on how they would be judged following Germany's defeat. Amidst the chaos of that journey it may have been possible for Bonhoeffer and the others to abscond, but they never did. Perhaps this is due to the others not been marked for execution. Bonhoeffer, by administrative error, had been sent with them to Regensburg and then Schonberg, when he should have been taken directly to Flossenburg for execution with other members of the conspiracy who had been directly transported there. Maybe at this stage Bonhoeffer thought the error would save him and that there was no need therefore to take the gamble of escape.

What was it that allowed Dietrich Bonhoeffer to see through the Nazi claims and be so resolute in his opposition to the Nazi regime when so many others, including those in the church, fell apparently spellbound beneath its ideological and even theological claims? Bonhoeffer was already a man of considerable international exposure and wide experience even before the advent of the Nazi regime. That international exposure and wide experience had begun on his above-mentioned trip to Italy, where aged just eighteen his eyes were opened to both the breadth of culture rooted in its Greaco-Roman foundations and universality of the church, a universality far removed from the narrow nationalism of so much of the nationalist Lutheran Church in Germany. Later in 1928 he would spend time in Barcelona as pastor to a German-speaking congregation, and though with a German expatriate congregation Bonhoeffer still had plenty of opportunities to imbibe the wider cultural tradition. His first trip to the United States, in 1930–31, was particularly crucial in opening Bonhoeffer's eyes to issues concerning race, which would become so central in his opposition to policies that the Nazis would enact. During his time there Bonhoeffer travelled to the segregated South and was appalled by the treatment of Blacks. He precipitously wrote of the racism he found in the U.S., in light of later events, that "our Jewish problem is a joke by comparison." His sensitivity to this racial treatment was raised by his befriending a fellow student at Union, Frank Fisher. Fisher was Black and took Bonhoeffer to the Abyssinian Baptist Church in Harlem, where Bonhoeffer fell in love with the Black gospel music he experienced there, and he took records of it back with him when he returned to Germany. But it was not only the music of that place that Bonhoeffer enjoyed. He found in the Black church a message full of passion and commitment so contrary to what he judged as the dry, dispassionate message he had received at Union and in the church at Riverside, to which Union was intimately related. In the Black church Bonhoeffer found what he judged to be a gospel message that spoke to him, linking both social justice concerns with an evangelical gospel.

Along with Frank Fisher, Bonhoeffer met three other students at Union who would play a major role in his life: the French Jean Lassere, the Swiss Erwin Sutz, and the American Paul Lehmann. Jean Lassere was highly influential in turning Bonhoeffer to a path of peace and non-violent resistance. While in New York Bonhoeffer viewed with Lassere the film *All Quiet on the Western Front*, and that viewing was perhaps the seminal point in Bonhoeffer being turned in that direction. The film was based on the book of the same name written by Erich Maria Remarque, which described the horrors on the First World War. It was among the first of the books consigned to the flames by the Nazis in the national book burnings of May 10, 1933. Lassere also encouraged Bonhoeffer to become involved in the nascent ecumenical movement, which would further open Bonhoeffer's eyes to the universal nature of the church and also prove invaluable in his later role as an Abwehr agent, both in his official and conspiratorial roles. Having met Lassere, Bonhoeffer was driven to follow up on the idea of non-violent resistance and thought then and numerous times later of visiting the man most associated with that movement, Mahatma Gandhi in India. The cost, however, was prohibitive so instead he joined Lassere and Lehmann in driving to Mexico. Lehmann left them before the border but Bonhoeffer and Lassere travelled on, logging some 1,200 miles in Mexico before returning. That experience in such a different culture again of course could not help but broaden Bonhoeffer's outlook.

That, however, was not the end of Bonhoeffer's international experience. Following the Nazis ascension to power in 1933 Bonhoeffer spent time serving in two London congregations, again made up of German expatriates. He had moved to London believing that a position in an overseas congregation would best allow him to have a platform from which he could intervene in the internal struggle within the German church as to policy toward the new Nazi government. Bonhoeffer's aim was to have the overseas German congregations leave the Reichskirche, believing this to be the best course of opposition. Bonhoeffer also tried to get the ecumenical movement to move to a place where it would recognise the Confessing Church rather than the Reichskirche as the true German church. During this sojourn in London Dietrich Bonhoeffer was also able to establish a friendship with Bishop George Bell, the bishop of Chichester for the Church of England. Bell had been present in Berlin at the time of a German Christian conference and, after hearing the shrill words of that group's leaders, had been resolutely opposed to the Nazi regime. Later during the war Bell would act as Bonhoeffer's conduit to the outside world, even making representation to the British government on matters brought to him by Bonhoeffer while he was operating as part of the conspiracy.

Recognising the danger of rival systems of thought, Hitler almost immediately upon coming to power sought the best way of making use of the churches, thereby muting any critique of his government they may offer. Though he had an antipathy to the church and indeed Christianity itself, he unlike others of the Nazis, realised the importance of keeping the churches onside and at least making pretence of having a favourable view of Christianity. His real philosophy of course was the worship of the Nietzschean "ubermensh" (the person asserting and using their own power), which he saw typified in the old German folk religions. With the aim of keeping the church onside, however, he moved within six months of coming to power to sign a concordat with the Vatican on July 20, 1933. Likewise, within months of coming to power he and the Nazis began to develop a method by which they could deal with the disparate Protestant churches. In order to best deal with these churches the Nazis encouraged moves to develop a centralised Reichskirche (a national church) headed by a Reichsbishof. The candidate put forward by the church was Friedrich von Bodelschwingh, who represented everything that the Nazis were not, having been ministering to a community of physically and intellectually handicapped people at Bethel in Westphalia—the type of people that the Nazis would soon begin exterminating as a drain on both the economy and purity of the Reich. In a matter of a few weeks von Bodelschwingh found the position untenable and resigned. Church elections were called for on July 23, 1933 and the successful candidate for the office of Reichsbishof, Ludwig Muller, was one much more amenable to the Nazis. With the election of Muller the German Christians reached their nadir in the church, and at the national synod on September 5, 1933 some 80 percent of the delegates wearing the brown shirts of the Nazis dominated the proceedings, leading the synod to be known as "the Brown Synod."

Bonhoeffer and a few others, Franz Hildebrandt among them, understood the danger of the church becoming completely aligned to the regime and began to draw up a document that would serve as the basis for the Pastors' Emergency League. By the end of the year it would have six thousand members.

Gradually Bonhoeffer arrived at the view that the Reichskirche was no longer church, its views and espoused doctrine being so contrary to both the gospel and historical church that it no longer merited being called church. Called back to Berlin from London by the head of the Reichskirche foreign office, Theodor Heckel, to be disciplined, including being forbidden being involved in any ecumenical activity, Bonhoeffer met with Martin Niemoller and Gerhard Jacobi to begin planning a complete break with the Reichskirche and the establishment of a "Confessing Church" in a gathering to be held at the end of May 1934 at Barmen. This was a step beyond the Pastors' Emergency League as it was now a clear break from rather than a reform movement from within the Reichskirche. From the Barmen meeting came the famous document establishing the Confessing Church and declaring the Reichskirche to be heretical for having broken with Christian doctrine and practice. By April the following year Bonhoeffer could write controversially that, "whoever knowingly separates themselves from the Confessing Church separates themselves from salvation."[10]

The broadening of Bonhoeffer's understanding allowed him to move further than nearly all others in both the church and Germany in general were prepared to go. The great majority of those even in the Confessing Church were not prepared to be involved in actions that may could be seen to be unpatriotic and so they held back from criticising Germany in the international arena. Germany after all, they judged, had been the victim of many of the nations of those making the criticisms at the end of the First World War with the Treaty of Versailles, and had not Hitler acted correctly in breaking that onerous and unfair treaty? The unjust nature of Versailles had been milked for all it was worth by the

---

10. Bonhoeffer, "Question of the Boundaries of the Church and the Church Union," lecture delivered April 24, 1936, quoted in Metaxas, *Bonhoeffer: Pastor, Martyr, Prophet, Spy* (Nashville: T. Nelson, 2010) 286.

Nazis and had largely been instrumental in their rise to power. Such a context made unpatriotic actions a step too far for those in the Confessing Church.

Following his recall to Germany from England by Martin Niemoller, the major part of Bonhoeffer's service with the Confessing Church was in his being the director of two theological seminaries, Zingst on the Baltic Sea and Finkenwalde in Pomerania in the far eastern part of Germany, followed by the "collective pastorates," after the Nazis had forcibly closed Finkenwalde. Niemoller and others had decided to take this course of action of establishing independent seminaries following the Nazi decree that all theological students within the university faculty would be required to prove their "Aryan purity."

The students who became part of these seminaries under Bonhoeffer found themselves experiencing something far different from the norm. Gone was a strict academic formality along with a dispassionate study of religion, and in their place came a community understanding whereby students, rather than addressing him as "Herr Direktor," were invited to call him "bruder," while rigorous academic study was accompanied by a deep piety and Christian community life together. Bonhoeffer insisted on prayer, mediation, confession, and worship all being equal parts of seminary life along with academic study. He reflected on this community life in the book *Life Together*. It was during his time at Finkenwalde that Bonhoeffer became particularly close with one of his students, Eberhard Bethge, who not only became very close to Bonhoeffer but also did much to foster the works and present the life of Bonhoeffer to the world following the end of the war. During their time together Bethge became not only Bonhoeffer's confidante but even his confessor.

Ultimately Bonhoeffer, although he was a major figure in its establishment, would see the limits of the Confessing Church opposition to the regime and move ever deeper into the underground activities of the conspiracy. Bethge was a witness to Bonhoeffer's crossing over from open non-violent resistance to the regime exercised from the Confessing Church to his covert conspiratorial actions within the Abwehr. That change happened on the day the French capitulated to the Nazis. Bethge was at a café with Bonhoeffer when the news came through and the response of all present was to stand and make the Nazi salute—Bonhoeffer among them. Bethge was horrified and admonished Bonhoeffer, who responded that the matter was not important. Clearly now working underground, Bonhoeffer no longer wished to draw attention and instead presented himself as a loyal member of the Abwehr working for the regime.

What drove Bonhoeffer into the conspiracy and to be involved in traitorous actions to his own nation? The first we have already mentioned: the lukewarm compromised stance of the Confessing Church. In a paper he wrote in 1935, "The Confessing Church and the Ecumenical Movement," he was highly critical of both the Confessing Church for its limiting of its opposition to the regime's intrusion into the ecclesiastical realm and of the ecumenical movement for its preparedness to continue to be engaged with the Reichskirche. His negative view of the Confessing Church was deepened when he learned that in response to the Nazi's "Nuremberg Laws" enacted September 15, 1935 the church was considering a resolution conceding the state's right to enact such draconian legislation at its upcoming synod. Although in the end the Confessing Church synod didn't accede to the resolution, it equally didn't take a stance in opposition to the legislation. Bonhoeffer, who had already seen the need to support the Jews and other opponents suffering at the hands of the Nazis, was particularly appalled.

The other reason Bonhoeffer moved on from the Confessing Church was the increasing inability and ineffectiveness of its opposition to the Nazis juggernaut. A case in point was the action of the Confessing Church to finally make its opposition to many Nazi policies in a document delivered to the Chancellery itself in June 1936. The idea was to bring Hitler and the Nazis "to the table" in the hope of moderating their behaviour. The document, however, was leaked to the international media in Britain and Switzerland, initially it was thought by the Nazis but later found to be by two of Bonhoeffer's former students, Werner Koch and Ernst Tillich. This action played into the Nazis hands, who, while riding at the peak of their popularity with the hosting of the Berlin Olympics, were able to portray the Confessing Church as traitorous. As their hold on power deepened the Nazis were also able to increasingly suppress the Confessing Church and silence any critique of the regime that it offered. Thus, during 1937 they were able to arrest over eight hundred pastors and other leaders of the Confessing Church, among them Martin Niemoller. Bonhoeffer and Bethge were visiting Berlin on July 1, 1937 and upon arriving at Niemoller's residence found that he had only just been arrested by the Gestapo, following which they were themselves held for a few hours under house arrest. Niemoller would not be released until he was freed by the Allies at the end of the war. Franz Hildebrandt stepped into Niemoller's parish to lead worship but he also was arrested after conducting a service on July 18, 1935. Great concern was held for him given his racial classification as a Jew by the Nazis. Hans von Dohnanyi through his contacts was able to win his release with Hildebrandt, immediately fleeing Germany for Britain through Switzerland. A few weeks later the Nazis again moved to silence the Confessing Church by closing the seminary at Finkenwalde, Bonhoeffer and Bethge learning this news while holidaying together. In January the following year Bonhoeffer was again arrested at a Confessing Church meeting in Dahlem. Clearly in Bonhoeffer's eyes it was becoming increasingly clear that it would require far more than the actions being taken by the Confessing Church to challenge and ultimately bring down the regime.

Growing disillusioned with the Confessing Church, by 1938 Bonhoeffer was becoming increasingly connected to the conspiratorial resistance. This connection was primarily through the familial link he had with his brother-in-law Hans von Dohnanyi, through whom he was becoming increasingly aware of the depth and extent of the evil acts being carried out by the Nazis. Dohnanyi had been compiling the Zossen files, which would ultimately lead to so many deaths among the conspirators, in which he carefully noted all the atrocities being carried out by the regime. Initially

Bonhoeffer was not fully involved in the conspiracy, more so being one providing spiritual counsel and support for those who were. The events of Kristallnacht, November 9–10, 1938, whereby the Nazis burned and demolished synagogues across the Reich and thereupon increased persecution of the Jewish populace, greatly effected Bonhoeffer, whose mediative text for the day included the line, "They burn all God's houses in the land" (Ps 74:8), which he marked in his Bible. Bonhoeffer's increasing horror at the crimes being perpetrated by the Nazis, in particular the events of Kristallnacht, led him to become increasingly involved with the conspiratorial resistance. His final decision to commit fully to the conspiracy was probably partly in response to words of challenge spoken to him by his sister-in-law Emmi, married to Dietrich's brother Klaus, that Christians were often paralysed into inaction due to their concern for their moral purity. "You Christians," she challenged, "are glad when someone else does what you know must be done, but it seems that you are unwilling to get your own hands dirty and do it." Such a challenge no doubt also further shaped Bonhoeffer's *Ethics*, on which he was still working.

The commencement of war meant that the Nazis now had absolute free reign to carry out their atrocities, especially in the east against the Poles and others they regarded as "untermenschen" (subhuman). Hans von Dohnanyi, of course, in his position was privy to the nature of the SS actions being carried out, and as he made these known to Bonhoeffer the Lutheran pastor was being inextricably drawn ever deeper into the conspiracy. That conspiracy was growing ever more extensively centred in the military, with many commanders being repulsed by the Nazi atrocities they had witnessed or heard of from their peers, feeling that the reputation of the Wehrmacht was being besmirched by its association with such crimes. These circles were increasingly feeling that a coup d'état was necessary. These officers included Admiral Canaris, the head of the Abwehr, who like many of the others had initially supported Hitler but became increasingly appalled by Nazi actions.

Being a member of the Abwehr was ideal for Bonhoeffer, for as far as the Nazis were concerned his ecumenical contacts would be beneficial for them as a part of military intelligence, while of course those same ecumenical links were invaluable in his real work as a conspirator. His joining the Abwehr was not however without difficulties. As Bethge had been horrified when Bonhoeffer first stood to give the Nazi salute, so now, with him seemingly working with the Nazi war machine, were many of his colleagues in the Confessing Church. They could not help but wonder if Bonhoeffer had passed over to the other side. How was it that he was receiving so many bounteous benefits, such as overseas travel in a time of war and exemption from military service, from the Nazis? Of course Bonhoeffer was unable to reveal his real motivation for his position and this must have pained him. Working through his conspiratorial role with the Abwehr, Bonhoeffer's role was to make contact with ecumenical leaders, who in turn could make contact with the political leaders in their own lands and let them know of the German resistance. The hope was that the political leadership in these lands would offer support to the conspirators in their plans for a coup d'état. For their part, the German resistance of course wanted a guarantee that any government succeeding the Nazis would not be burdened with onerous conditions such as those placed on Germany at the end of the previous war. Bishop George Bell was central to these links with the British government and Bonhoeffer was able to meet with him a number of times on his overseas trips on behalf of the Abwehr. Bell, from the time of his being appalled by the crudity of the German Christians on a visit to Berlin, had resolutely opposed the Nazis and as a Church of England bishop was a member of the House of Lords, therefore having extensive contacts with the British political leadership. On numerous occasions Bell presented the case of the German conspirators to the British government, but to no avail. British public opinion, fostered by Prime Minister Winston Churchill in particular, having made the equation that "all Germans were Nazis," was decidedly antithetical to any German entreaty and instead was set on pursuing total victory. It is a moot point to wonder how many millions of lives could have been saved if such support had been given to the conspiracy from the earliest of days, when the Nazis were most vulnerable.

Dietrich Bonhoeffer's first serious assignment for the resistance working through the Abwehr was in an operation codenamed U7, whereby seven Jews would be assisted to leave Germany, ostensively with the task of informing the world just how well the Jewish populace was being treated in Germany. Bonhoeffer's initial imprisonment along with that of Hans von Dohnanyi in the military prison at Tegel was the result of this Abwehr operation and the suspicions it raised within the Gestapo. Switzerland, the place to where the Jews were being smuggled, demanded a large payment for the transaction, with the result being that currency irregularities were uncovered by a customs officer, which led to Wilhelm Schmidhuber, a member of the Abwehr. Under torture at the hands of the Gestapo, he leaked information leading to General Oster and Hans von Dohnanyi, and from them the trail led to Bonhoeffer. Along with their natural antipathy to the Abwehr as competitors in the intelligence field, the Gestapo also had long held suspicions about the Abwehr and this was their ideal opportunity to emasculate it.

As to the Jews, the reality of course was that their position in the Reich and in the territory it controlled was rapidly deteriorating. In the east they were being massacred and now had to wear a yellow star at all times. The increasing oppression of the Jewish populace of course climaxed in the Shoah or Holocaust, the "Final Solution" that had been set in place at the Wannsee Conference on January 20, 1942.

With the arrests and the possibility that the Abwehr complicity in the conspiracy could soon be uncovered, the attempts to assassinate Hitler now intensified, first with what is known as the Schlabrendorff Plot, when a bomb disguised as a bottle of brandy failed to detonate while being carried aboard Hitler's plane on March 13, 1943, followed by another attempt planned for March 21 when the unholy triumvirate of Hitler, Himmler, and Goering would be together at an armaments inspection. That attempt would involve suicide for Major General Randolf Christoph von

Gersdorff, who would detonate a bomb he was wearing under his coat. The bomb was triggered but Hitler shortened the inspection and left before the time set for detonation.

Time had run out, however, for Bonhoeffer and the other Abwehr conspirators. On April 5, 1943 Bonhoeffer called the von Dohnanyi home but the phone was answered by an unfamiliar voice. The Gestapo were already at the residence and Hans had been placed under arrest. Bonhoeffer rushed to put his papers in order seeking to hide his complicity in the conspiratorial circle and then went next door to the Schleicher residence. At 4 p.m. his father Karl arrived to tell him there were two men waiting to speak with him. One of these men was Judge Advocate Manfred Roeder. Taken away in a black Mercedes, Dietrich Bonhoeffer was never again to return home. Initially it seemed likely that Bonhoeffer and the others arrested in his circle would escape detection concerning the depths of their activities against the Nazis. It was decided that Hans von Dohnanyi would bear the brunt of the questioning while Bonhoeffer would play the naïve pastor. Their stories were harmonised by means of an elaborate system whereby coded messages were passed through books delivered to Tegel by the family. This involved tiny dots being placed under letters that when read backwards formed messages. When the head of the Abwehr, Admiral Wilhelm Canaris, who had been covering for them, was arrested in February 1944, things began to turn for the worse. A few months later the failure of the von Stauffenberg plot and discovery of the Zossen files would condemn Bonhoeffer and many in the Abwehr circle to their grisly end. That end for Bonhoeffer would begin when he was taken from his cell at Tegel and transferred to the Gestapo's Prinz-Albrecht-Strasse prison.

We know little of Bonhoeffer from the time of his arrival at Prinz-Albrecht-Strasse. His correspondence ceased and visits were not permitted. Fabian von Schlabrendorff tells us something of him in his *I Knew Dietrich Bonhoeffer*, mentioning his bravery, his care for other prisoners, and how even in this place he was able to win some of the guards over. He also tells us that von Dohnanyi was so severely tortured he had a stroke by which he was blinded.

Bonhoeffer still sought to conceal his involvement but relented when threats were made concerning his family and fiancé, at which point he declared himself to be an enemy of National Socialism. On February 2 the notorious Roland Freisler in the "People's Court" sentenced to death his brother and brother-in-law, Klaus Bonhoeffer and Rudiger Schleicher, and was about to condemn von Schlabrendorff to similar fate the following day when a massive air raid over Berlin carried out by almost one thousand B-17 Flying Fortresses saw three thousand bombs fall on the stricken city. One of them found Roland Freisler's courtroom, killing him and ensuring the survival of von Schlabrendorff.

On February 7 Dietrich Bonhoeffer and another nineteen prominent prisoners were moved from Prinz-Albrecht-Strasse to the concentration camps of Buchenwald and Flossenburg, with Bonhoeffer being sent to the former. One of those with Bonhoeffer at Buchenwald was the British Intelligence Officer S. Payne Best, who wrote of Bonhoeffer, "He was one of the very few men that I have met to whom his God was real and ever close to him." With the sound of Allied shells in the distance on April 3, 1945, sixteen of the prisoners including Bonhoeffer were packed into a van meant for only eight and transported south. At one point the journey was halted and three prisoners were taken off to be sent to Flossenburg. The other thirteen continued on the journey. With no fuel left the Nazis were reduced to using wood for fuel, and the fumes filled the passenger cabin during the long thirteen-hour journey. With daylight fading, the group with their three SS guards spent the night at a state prison at Regensburg, where the prisoners found many of the family members of those involved in the July 20 plot. In the meantime a significant part of Canaris's diary had been found at Zossen on April 4, 1945. Hitler, on reading it the following day, condemned all those named in it to death. The next afternoon Bonhoeffer and his fellow prisoners were again moved, but after just a few miles the truck in which they were travelling broke down and they spent the entire night in it before the guards flagged down a bus the next morning. That evening the group arrived at Schonberg, where they found the others whom they had left at Regensburg. The night preceding his been taken from Schonberg it seems that Bonhoeffer enjoyed himself more than he had for a long time, engaging in a night of frivolity and enjoying the luxury of a proper bed in what had been a girl's infirmary in the school of that town. The next morning he conducted worship and upon concluding it was immediately taken away by two Gestapo agents sent to rectify the earlier mistake of Bonhoeffer not being separated out with the others to be sent to Flossenburg. Departing to his fate to Payne Best, Bonhoeffer stated, "This is the end, for me the beginning of life." That night he arrived at Flossenburg, where following a cursory trial he was court-martialled and sentenced to die, with that sentence being carried out the next morning, April 9, 1945.

At Flossenburg the prison camp doctor, H. Fischer-Hullstrung, observed Bonhoeffer in his last moments of life, writing of him,

> Through the open door in one room of the huts I saw Pastor Bonhoeffer before taking off his prison garb, kneeling on the floor praying fervently to his God. I was most deeply moved by the way this loveable man prayed, so devout and so certain that God heard his prayer. At the place of execution, he again said a short prayer and then climbed the steps to the gallows, brave and composed. His death ensued after a few seconds. In the almost fifty years that I have worked as a doctor, I have hardly ever seen a man die so entirely submissive to the will of God.[11]

---

11. Quoted in Metaxas, *Bonhoeffer*, 532.

BONHOEFFER
Prophet and Martyr

A play by John Queripel

List of Characters

Bonhoeffer—Pastor Dietrich Bonhoeffer

Paula Bonhoeffer—Mother of Dietrich Bonhoeffer

Karl Bonhoeffer—Father of Dietrich Bonhoeffer

Radio announcer for the Berlin Broadcasting Company

Bethge—Student and friend of Dietrich Bonhoeffer

Gerhard Leibhotz—Husband of Dietrich Bonhoeffer's twin sister, Sabine

Sabine Liebhotz—Twin sister of Dietrich Bonhoeffer

Bell—George, bishop of the Church of England, long-time ecumenical contact who made representations for the conspirators to the British government

Von Dohnanyi—Hans, husband of Dietrich Bonhoeffer's sister Christine, employed in the Ministry of Justice and a fellow conspirator

Von Kleist Retzow—Ruth, friend and patron of Dietrich Bonhoeffer

Von Wedemeyer—Fiancée of Dietrich Bonhoeffer, granddaughter of Ruth von Kleist Retzow

Beck—General Ludwig Beck, one of the chief conspirators in the attempts to kill Hitler

Ostler—Hans Ostler, one of the leaders in military security, fellow conspirator

Conspirator 1

Conspirator 2

Conspirator 3

Rudiger Schleiecher—Husband of Dietrich Bonhoeffer's sister Ursula, a lawyer and fellow conspirator

Klaus Bonhoeffer—Brother of Dietrich Bonhoeffer, a lawyer and fellow conspirator

Ursula Schleiecher—Sister of Dietrich Bonhoeffer, wife of fellow conspirator Rudiger Schleicher

Officer 1—Agent of the Reich's security office, the Gestapo

Officer 2—Agent of the Reich's security office, the Gestapo

Roeder—Judge Advocate Manfred Roeder

Knobloch—A corporal, Dietrich Bonhoeffer's guard and a conduit for uncensored correspondence; a working-class North Berlin man, of whom nothing was heard after the entry of the Soviet Army into Berlin

Radio Announcer for the British Broadcasting Commission

Act 1

SCENE 1

Stockholm, in the quarters of Bishop George Bell, 1 June 1942. Bell pours a whisky.

Bell: This Hitler is insane, a madman, a . . .

Bonhoeffer: If only he could be so easily dismissed. Do you think a whole nation would blindly follow one just simply mad, an escapee from some asylum? No. Hitler is cunning, devious, and clever—yes George, clever. He draws from a dark side of history, a side we, bathed in the Enlightenment and rationality, would rather ignore. Not everyone, however, bathes in such clear waters.

Bell: True, true, Dietrich, but surely you must take your opportunity to escape from the clutches of this . . . demonic tyrant.

Bonhoeffer: That I could, but you know for me that is not an option.

Bell: Dietrich, of course it is an option. You are safe here now. You don't have to return to Germany.

Bonhoeffer: I know very well I don't have to return to Germany, but I must return to Germany. There is a difference.

Bell: But you have everything to live for. I am sure you know the great danger in which you are placing yourself if you return. The church after this war will so need leaders like you, Dietrich. And I know a whole host of academic posts will open for you. What you are currently exploring, experiencing—your writings—must not be allowed to die with you. Your theological work is profound and will grow ever more so. It can't be thrown away. The ecumenical movement, the role it must play in rehabilitating Europe after the war . . .

Bonhoeffer: George, you make it sound as though I won't be around. I have no plans for dying. Martyrdom holds no sort of romantic ideal about it for me.

Bell: But you must know on what thin ice you are walking with this double play of yours.

Bonhoeffer: We—all of us in the resistance—are walking on the same thin ice, and we are no saints. Why, some of us don't even write tomes on ethics, God, meaning, purpose.

Bell: But Dietrich . . .

Bonhoeffer: No George! If I am to be truly ethical, to truly do God's will, be Christ's disciple, what is my option? I know God can choose as the divine instruments those who make no mention of his name, those whose ethics are questionable, but do you really think that I, who speaks so much of God, of costly discipleship, of ethics, can just opt out and leave what must be done to others?

Bell: But these means of which you have spoken; you place your very moral being in danger.

Bonhoeffer: So now am I to keep my pious hands clean, allow others to do the dirty work? All for the purity of my soul, my clear and clean conscience, that Christian pacifism be affirmed? No George, I will not, and if I go to hell for it, so be it!

Bell: Admirable, all very admirable, Dietrich, but let us be level-headed about all this. You risk throwing all this away; a future that can not only bring you great prestige, but that is so needed, especially when this war is ended and there will be so much reconstruction needing to be done.

Bonhoeffer: Exactly, George, and how can I be involved in the reconstruction of Germany after the war if I am not present in her darkest hour?

Bell: And if you do not survive?

Bonhoeffer: Well, I have never found the urge for self-preservation, for survival, when faced with the need to stand for truth, to be at the heart of our faith.

Bell: True, but unfair, Dietrich. You know that I only have your best interests at heart, but also the interests of not only our movement, but of the whole future in mind when I urge you to consider what I am saying.

Bonhoeffer: Of course I know that, George. A man could hardly have a greater friend than I have in you, and that you have my best interests at heart is precisely why it makes what you are saying all the more tempting and difficult to resist. It is not that I want to return to Germany but rather that I must.

Bell: So you cannot be tempted?

Bonhoeffer: No, George, I cannot.

Act 2

SCENE 1

The Bonhoeffer residence, 1 February 1933, two days after Hitler's installation as Chancellor.

Paula Bonhoeffer: Come, Karl, away from your books. It's almost time for Dietrich's presentation on the radio. Fancy our son being chosen to be heard all over Germany.

Karl Bonhoeffer: Well its one piece of good in these days. Have you the radio tuned?

Paula Bonhoeffer: Of course: Berlin Broadcasting Company. (Gets up and turns on radio. Radio is playing Wagner.)

Radio host: And that was from Richard Wagner's 'The Ring.' And how appropriate in honour of our new Fuhrer, Adolf Hitler, a great devotee of the German music of Wagner.
    And now the Berlin Broadcasting Company is pleased to present a talk from one of our nation's finest young theologians, Pastor Dietrich Bonhoeffer. Pastor Bonhoeffer was born in 1906 to a prominent Berlin family. His father, Karl Bonhoeffer, is Professor of Psychiatry and Neurology at the University of

Berlin, and as for his brothers, Karl-Friedrich is a fine physicist predicted to bring Germany great glory in the field, while Klaus is a lawyer. Even his sisters share in the family's intellectual riches. Ursula, married to Rudinger Schleicher, also a lawyer, is herself trained in social and educational studies. Christine, married to Hans von Dohnanyi, serving in the Ministry of Justice, has studied biology. Pastor Bonhoeffer's twin sister, Sabine, is married to Gerhard Leibholz, a constitutional lawyer, while the youngest of the sisters, Suzanne, shares her brother's interests in the church and theology. The family has also given of their blood for our dear Fatherland, Walter, the eldest of the brothers, having fallen giving his life in defence of the German nation in the Great War.

Pastor Dietrich Bonhoeffer studied theology at Tubingen, has completed a one-year scholarship at the Union Theological College in the United States of America, has served as a pastor overseas in London and Barcelona, and also has extensive international church experience through his service in the ecumenical movement, most recently representing Germany at the World Alliance Conference in Cambridge in the United Kingdom.

Herr Bonhoeffer is a man who certainly typifies and exemplifies the rigorous German mind and discipline. By the age of just twenty-one he had completed his doctorate. The new Germany rewards such and his future would seem to have no limit. Today he will address us on 'The younger generation's view of the concept of leader,' a most opportune topic when all of Germany is celebrating the elevation of Adolf Hitler to the rank of Chancellor just two days ago.

Bonhoeffer: Tonight I have been invited to speak to you about the concept of leader. What do we mean as a Christian when we say 'leader'? Who is our leader and what is the nature of leadership?

From the time of the Reformation here in Germany we have established a belief, which we have rigorously held, that there are two spheres of God's activity. These represent two kingdoms, related but each independent of the other. God is the ruler over both but chooses different instruments through whom he rules. In the temporal or secular realm God has chosen to rule through the civil authorities, while in the realm of the sacred God chooses to rule through the church. Each realm has its distinct place and each exists independent of the other. Each contains within it that which we call leadership, a leadership that is to lead in such manner that it seeks the best in the realm for which it is responsible, as is the will of God. Leadership in each is limited to its proper domain; that of the civil authorities to matters of the state, that of the ecclesiastical authorities to those affairs of the church. Neither should seek to extend its power and authority to that realm not proper to it. Given this, there is no leader whose leadership is absolute. For any leader to proclaim or so act in a manner that shows them claiming such is clearly outside that which is permissible.

Ultimately, the only one who can claim absolute leadership and therefore obedience for the Christian is Jesus Christ. In him both those spheres of which I have been speaking find their genesis. In him both spheres are established and each owes ultimate allegiance only to him. He is the only true and absolute leader in either sphere, and any other claims to absolute leadership must be named for what they are—idolatry.

In this moment of great change in our land we need to be more aware than ever about the nature of power, the temptation of temporal leadership to make claims for itself beyond that which is legitimate.

Leadership that claims for itself any absolute role must be resisted. I fear there are those in our land who would make such an extravagant claim of absolute power for our present leader.

If the leader allows himself to be persuaded by those he leads who want to turn him into their idol—and there are those who always hope for this—then the image of the leader will degenerate into that of the 'misleader.' The leader who makes an idol of himself and his office makes a mockery of God.

These claims need be . . .

Radio Host: Unfortunately we have found it necessary to terminate the lecture by Herr Bonhoeffer. Such talk has no place in the new Germany with its new leader, Adolf Hitler.

(Darkness falls. Horst Wessel is heard.)

SCENE 2

Finkenwalde Seminary, Bonhoeffer's room.

Bonhoeffer: I love this. The Black music of the United States has such life, such power. When it speaks of faith it truly sings! One hears the chains being lifted and broken. Eberhard, listen for something entirely different and let your soul be deeply moved. (Places record of Paul Robeson on the turntable. Listens and then begins to sing along.)

Bethge: My English is not as good as yours, Dietrich, but you are right. It is new to me, and yes, I do like it.

Act 2

Bonhoeffer: (Laughing) I'm glad you do. You know, this Robeson—a giant of a man in every way. When he was younger at college, though he was very good at the game they refused to pick him for the college American football team. You know why? He was Black. Purely because of his race! To judge a man by his race—how stupid, how ignorant! So you know what Robeson did? He picked up that coach in a great bear hug (demonstrates) and was threatening to throw him down when suddenly that coach cried out, 'Robeson, you're in, you're in the team.' (Laughs heartily.) I know that doesn't fit very well with the pacifism I am expounding these days, but I like that story very much.

Eberhard, the Black church in the U.S. can hardly be believed. Such celebration, such life, such joy, but all so rooted in that costly discipleship of which I have spoken and written about. The situation of the Negros in the U.S. is terrible. Everywhere they are second-class citizens. In the South they have their own separate place in a bar or restaurant, separate from White people. They must use a separate toilet, drink from a different tap. They risk being lynched for any reason by White vigilantes, who are beyond the law, or who perhaps are the law.

Bethge: Reminds one of the situation here.

Bonhoeffer: Indeed it does. When I went to Union Theological Seminary it was a Black fellow student with whom I felt I had the most in common. Many times I accompanied him to the Abyssinian Baptist Church in Harlem, the Negro ghetto in New York. Such worship you couldn't believe—the singing, the music . . . and the preaching. The call for commitment, to truly follow Jesus, so clear.

Bethge: And here, Dietrich? To follow Jesus...

Bonhoeffer: To follow Jesus now in Germany is to heed his call to pacifism: 'blessed are the peacemakers.' It is imperative we heed this call. Yet is so difficult for many to hear. Even here in the seminary there is a celebration when Hitler announces compulsory military service. The students celebrate! How silenced is the call of Jesus mid the clamour of war. When I speak against the new law it is as though I am ignored, or worse still, viewed as a traitor. But are we not traitorous—traitors to Christ—when we so easily vest ourselves of a uniform and go marching off to war?

Bethge: You are right, but can we expect more? We have allowed our church, even the gospel itself, to become so enmeshed with the interests of the state that it becomes almost impossible to distinguish the two. Hitler and the Nazis call the church 'meekly follows.'

Bonhoeffer: And leaves the gospel! Pacifism—the pacifism of the Gospels—is a lesson I have had to learn. I remember first meeting a French man, Jean Laussere, and hearing of it. We travelled down from the United States to Mexico. What conversations we had. How much he taught me! It was all new, Eberhard, so inoculated have we become to the way of a violent gospel. 'But Dietrich,' he would say, '"Blessed are the peacemakers, for theirs is the kingdom of Heaven." Can there be a clearer call?' How shameful I felt for my blindness. 'You cannot absent the political sphere from the gospel demand,' he'd say. It was he and others who introduced me to the thinking of Mahatma Gandhi—non-violent struggle against wrong, the true power of pacifism. You know, I want to go to India and meet and learn from this remarkable man.

ACT 2

Bethge: India!

Bonhoeffer: Yes. I even have two bishops, Martin Niemoller here and George Bell in England, working on getting me an invitation. I hope to sail soon. What an experience that will be. This man is truly a prophet. He understands, though he calls himself not a Christian, the way of Christ better than those who so call themselves but yet are ever ready to put on jackboots and go off to war singing the hymns of Christ, invoking God's blessing and blessed by our churches, blind to the call of Jesus.

Bethge: But Dietrich, you demand so much. The law of military service is absolute. There are no exemptions. What if you are called?

Bonhoeffer: I can only hope that God will give me the power to refuse.

Bethge: You know the punishment for refusal?

Bonhoeffer: I do. And that is why I can only ask for God's grace and strength.

SCENE 3

Sounds of smashing glass and angry voices calling 'Juden sweinhund,' etc.

Bonhoeffer: And so it has come. The insanity has no more discretion left at all. It bares openly the logic of its madness. It began with the burning of books and now the burning of synagogues. With what shall it end?

Bethge: The Jews are an accursed people; judgment always weighed upon them.

Bonhoeffer: The judgment weighed upon them is our judgment, not that of God's as we would like to have. Our judgment is their curse. It is not some abstract thing but is a concrete reality from our 'Christian' hand. We are responsible. It is by our complicit silence that it has come to this. The church should have thundered in defence of Christ's own people. You may put all sorts of reasoning around it, Eberhard, but our silence is the silence of cowardice and unbelief.

Bethge: But what chance now to protest? There can be no protest in this Germany. Everyone has been silenced—an intimidation of fear.

Bonhoeffer: True, there is no room left now for the normal channels of protest. It is too late for that, but earlier, earlier when there was still air to breathe . . . You remember, Eberhard, when those stupid anti-Jewish measures began, over five years ago with the store boycott. Courage was needed, nothing more than the courage to stand. I remember my grandmother, an aged woman. Those Nazi thugs, they stood at the door of the shop where she always went and tried to stop her entering. 'This is a Jewish store,' they said, 'and there is a German boycott today.' She had none of it. She wanted her groceries, especially her strawberries, 'Mr. Rosen has the best strawberries—so sweet.' She always bought her strawberries there and no state sanction, especially one so stupid, was going to stop her. And it didn't. Those two men stood aside and in she went. You see, all that was needed was courage then, and the whole bluff would have been called and the edifice crumbled. But it is too late for that now. A different sort of courage

ACT 2

will be called for now. (Picks up a Bible and looks for Psalm 74.)

'Thy foes have roared in the midst of thy holy place and they set up their own signs for signs. At the upper entrance they hacked the wooden trellis with axes. And then all its carved wood they broke down with hatchets and hammers. They set thy sanctuary of fire. To the ground they desecrated the dwelling place of thy name. They said to themselves, "we will utterly subdue them." They burned all the meeting places of God in the land.'

Psalm 74, Eberhard. The houses of God, the synagogues, are burning. (Goes back to reading.) 'There are no longer any prophets. . . . How long is the foe to scoff? Is the enemy to revile thy name forever?'

SCENE 4

The Leibholz residence, November 1938.

Bonhoeffer: Sabine, Gerhard, it pains me to tell you but I pray that you will follow my advice. You must flee Germany. I know this comes as terrible news, but believe me you have no option. It is far too dangerous here. Kristalnacht is just the beginning. Nothing can protect you—not family connection, not profession—nothing! You are Jewish and that is all that matters to these mad men. The Nazis have no places for Jews in their 'new Germany.'

Gerhard Leibhotz: But surely, Dietrich, the madness will pass. Surely . . .

Bonhoeffer: It will not pass till these mad men wreak far more havoc yet. This has become far more than discriminatory laws, themselves bad enough. More even than the burning of synagogues! Hitler is planning a new Germany, a new Europe 'cleansed' of the Jews he calls vermin. Already camps are being established, and not just for political prisoners but for whole peoples—Jews, Gypsies, Communists the insane. Just being a Jew is to be subhuman, and being subhuman in their Germany is a crime.

Sabine Liebhotz: But Dietrich, that is mad, totally irrational.

Bonhoeffer: There is no rationality left in Germany. We should have seen it from the beginning. Hitler, after all, was at least honest. He made his intentions clear. It was all in *Mein Kampf*. Straightaway on coming to power he deprived the Jews of their citizenship, and it's gotten worse from there. Did we think he was suddenly going to recant and change his mind? Once a people is no longer a people they are but 'pests' to be exterminated.

Gerhard Leibhotz: Exterminated! Surely you exaggerate. Not even Hitler . . .

Bonhoeffer: Yes he can, will, and already is even now. The Einsatzgruppen are already killing your people. Your people, Gerhard, are being rounded up for no reason other than that they are Jews and being eliminated. They are shot, Gerhard, and buried in mass graves. And Hitler plans worse once war breaks out. They don't try to hide it. They even boast of it! The SS speaks of the total annihilation of the Jews if war breaks out. Haven't you read *Das Schwarze Korps*?

Sabine Leibhotz: But Dietrich, how can you know all this? Are you sure?

Act 2

Bonhoeffer: Hans and I have been talking. Military Intelligence has information and he asked me to warn you. He assures me there is no doubting the veracity of the information they have.

(Silence)

Gerhard Leibhotz: But how? How do we leave? The Nazis are not about to let us flee if they want to round us up to exterminate us.

Bonhoeffer: Hans can get some papers, papers that will enable you to leave Germany safely.

Gerhard Leibhotz: But surely you endanger both of yourselves.

Bonhoeffer: Gerhard, it is the least I can do. I have failed you previously preferring safety when I should have had the courage to do what was right.

Gerhard Leibhotz: The funeral?

Bonhoeffer: Yes, your father's funeral and my refusal to take part because I was advised I should not as he was Jewish. I was a coward and I can never express how sorry I am, but my time of cowardice is hopefully over.

Sabine Leibhotz: Past, Dietrich; finished, forgiven, and forgotten. Let us deal with what is before us now. You are absolutely sure we must leave?

Bonhoeffer: Thank you, Sabine. And as for you fleeing, yes, I am absolutely sure and we need to move quickly. Even with connections there are only a few that can be moved.

Sabine Leibhotz: Gerhard, I am sure we must trust Dietrich's judgment, and that of Hans.

(Silence)

Gerhard Leibhotz: (Angrily) Curse this Hitler, these damn Nazis. Everything—everything is gone!

Bonhoeffer: And we can save only that which is left: both your lives. Thank God for Hans and his contacts in Military Intelligence. Duplicity and lies will allow us the moral act.

SCENE 5

Bonhoeffer in a pulpit.

Bonhoeffer: We shall not shirk from the word 'pacifism.' The next war must be outlawed by our obedience to a command of God that is aimed at us today, namely, that there shall be no more war, because it blinds us to revelation. As a branch of ecumenism the World Council has heard God's call to peace and directs his command to the peoples of the world. Our theological task here therefore consists solely in hearing this commandment as a binding commandment and not discussing it as an open question. Who gives the call to peace so that the world hears it, so that the world is forced to hear it, so that all the nations have to rejoice? The individual Christian cannot do it. Only the one great ecumenical council of Christ's holy church throughout the world can proclaim it, so that the world, gnashing its teeth, has to hear the word of peace, and so that the nations rejoice because the church of Christ takes the weapons out of the children's hands in the name of Christ and

ACT 2

forbids the war and shouts out the peace of Christ over the raging world. The hour is at hand. The world bristles with weapons. The fanfares of war could be sounded tomorrow. Why are we still waiting? Do we ourselves want to be guilty too, guilty as never before?

SCENE 6

Following delivery of Bonhoeffer's sermon.

Bell: Well spoken, Dietrich. You certainly have left no one in any ambiguity as to your stance and the stance the church must take.

Bonhoeffer: But do you think they heard me, really heard me?

Bell: I am sure they have.

Bonhoeffer: You English—always so optimistic! I wish I could share that optimism.

Bell: We must not despair. That will get us nowhere, Dietrich.

Bonhoeffer: But George, the church is so lost. The voice of Christ is so muted. In Germany those of us who are faithful to his voice have been driven out of the church. The German Christians with more loyalty to Hitler than to Christ hold every position. The symbol they use tells all: the swastika superimposed over the cross of Christ! Even the Confessing Church has been compromised. What did Barmen achieve? A declaration full of good words and intent, or was it even that? An attempt to preserve the realm of the church as immune from the claims of the state. 'Do whatever you like to whomever you like, as long as we are left undefiled by your atrocities and can carry out our religious duties.' So we pray and we preach while outside there is absolute brutality, arbitrary detention and imprisonment of any who don't show themselves to be good Nazis. Self-interest and let the world go to hell. Dare we play at some pretence of keeping ecclesiastical purity when the world is going to hell? No! We must be as immersed in our world as the one we profess to follow was immersed in the world. Only then are we faithful.

Bell: This is the power of the ecumenical movement, the commitment to a church faithful to the way of Christ beyond all national and confessional bounds.

Bonhoeffer: Then why do we so often fail? George, we must examine the reality, not live in the ideal. The German church is no longer the church of Jesus Christ but the church of the Nazi party. Hitler, faced with some opposition, timid though it was, from the Confessing Church, sets up the 'Church Committees,' all in the name of reasonableness of course. The German Christians, the Confessing Church, and neutrals all brought together, and establishes a 'Church Ministry.' And what does the Confessing Church do? Falls prey to this predator. Innocent and naive, full of ideals but lacking any conviction and courage, it backs down to this demand.

Over and over, the Enabling Act, the Aryan Paragraph, the Civil Service Restoration Act, the Nuremberg Laws—all met with mute silence from the church.

Bell: Surely, Dietrich, it can't be all as bad as you paint it. What of the Pastors' Emergency League?

Bonhoeffer: Not enough! The Jews, George—to be Jewish is itself a crime in Germany. Jesus Christ would be chased out of Germany, or arrested, killed! And you know, George, that the majority of the church would quietly stand by and allow that to happen, or worse still would hand him over, all in the name of being good citizens, of being good Christians.

Bell: But surely, Dietrich, Hitler will go too far, alienate too many and his edifice will fall.

Bonhoeffer: If only it were so. The Nazi's power allows for no protest, no dissent. Everyone, every institution has been brought to heel. All are silenced. There are no civil institutions, no political parties, no trade unions who can speak. The military swear a personal oath to Hitler himself, and the church, the last organisation that could speak—both Protestant and Catholic—has sold itself, and not even for thirty pieces of silver. Those representing Germany in this ecumenical movement cannot be called Christians; they do not follow Christ. At best we are silent, at worst complicit.

Bell: But Germany has such a rich Christian culture. Surely that at some stage will reassert itself and bring all this madness to and end.

Bonhoeffer: That so-called Christian culture is the problem. That word 'culture' is everywhere in Germany. German culture is Christian culture, we are assured; the two are synonymous. And we have allowed it to happen. It is as though we have baptised a whole culture and nation, and in so doing have allowed that nation and culture in the name of Christ to do whatever it likes. Intoning Luther's 'sola fide,' faith alone, we have doled out grace so cheaply—worse than that, given it away—nothing asked for, nothing demanded, all free. Take it and sanctify your odorous actions. *The Cost of*

Discipleship—I may as well not have bothered writing it.

Bell: The Jews. What is happening?

Bonhoeffer: Silence, George, deafening silence. Not a voice is raised. Not even after Kristalnacht did even the Confessing Church utter a sound. A few mute protests about them taking 'our Jews,' those who have been baptised and joined the church, but that is all. Nothing more. We want to care for 'our Jews.' 'Don't touch them. They are ours. Stay out of the church realm.' We pathetically attempt to defend our own realm. And then we can't even do that as the Nazis drag them out of our very congregations. Not even their conversion can save them. To the Nazis they were and are Jews. We wring our hands and do nothing. As for the Jews in general, we—worse than wringing our hands—wash them of the problem. You know, by the laws passed in Germany, Christ's people are outcasts. They are boycotted, suffer the indignity of a plethora of laws that discriminate against them, even strip them of their citizenship. They are brutalised and tormented, blamed for every problem.

Of course we do nothing. Anti-Semitism has marked our church—and not only in Germany—for centuries. Hitler didn't just pluck it out of the air. It has been well cultivated in sacred ground. His brand of it is merely more virulent, given justification by what preceded it. Yet another failure of our 'Christian culture.'

Bell: You berate yourself and the German church mercilessly, Dietrich . . .

Act 2

Bonhoeffer: A good deal less mercilessly than God shall. God is not to be mocked, and we make a mockery of God with our pious silence. It is not our irreligiousness that is disobedience to God, but the fact that we are very glad to be religious. We are very glad when some government proclaims the 'Christian' attitude to life. The more pious we are, the less we have to tell ourselves God is dangerous. God is not to be mocked.

Act 3

SCENE 1

Bonhoeffer playing piano. Von Dohnanyi enters.

Von Dohnanyi: If I may interrupt something of beauty in these times of anything but . . .

Bonhoeffer: You honour me too greatly; any beauty is all that of the composer and not of the one playing.

Von Dohnanyi: Bach's B minor Mass. You see, some of us lawyers are somewhat appreciative of culture.

Bonhoeffer: (Laughs.) True. Not only theologians are called to higher things. But yes, the B minor Mass is one of my favourites. It allows me some inner peace in such times.

Von Dohnanyi: Higher things! (Laughing) But sometimes these higher things may involve us doing things here below. True? The ascent to those higher things calls us to start from the valley and thence again to return—the transfiguration, Dietrich?

ACT 3

Bonhoeffer Why Hans, do we make a theologian out of you yet? And here was I thinking it was Bach you had come to discuss.

Von Dohnanyi: (Suddenly serious) Dietrich, it is for you that I seek a career change. All your church contacts among the Allies can be of great worth both actively and as a cover.

Bonhoeffer: What do you mean?

Von Dohnanyi: Military intelligence, the Abwehr. I am proposing that we find you a position.

Bonhoeffer: Me, a theologian, as a spy? (Laughing) Come on, Hans!

Von Dohnanyi: Well, not quite. But Dietrich, you have many connections, connections that will make it easy enough for us to justify a placement for you in the Abwehr, and connections that will serve other uses over time.

Bonhoeffer: And you are now making a subversive of me? A traitor?

Von Dohnanyi: You know as well as I that in times such as these it is the subversive, the traitor, who is truly the patriot.

Bonhoeffer: But Hans, I am a theologian!

Von Dohnanyi: Too heavenly minded to be of earthly good.

Bonhoeffer: Unfair. That's unfair.

Von Dohnanyi: True, Dietrich, unfair for you. For most of the church fair comment, but yes unfair for you. 'A spoke in the wheel,' if I remember it right. There are times when the role of the church is to put a spoke in the wheel of the state when it does wrong. You see I do read your work.

Bonhoeffer: And this network: Who? How large? What influence?

Von Dohnanyi: So many questions. Do I detect an interest? For now, let me just say extensive, including the military—significant figures in the military.

Bonhoeffer: Then you are speaking of violence. You plan a violent overthrow of the Nazis? A coup d'état?

Von Dohnanyi: Can you suggest any other way? When all other methods are closed off, silenced by the state, then it becomes the duty of the few to make recourse to the only action that can work.

Bonhoeffer: And I'm to be involved—the theologian who made his reputation in the ecumenical movement speaking of pacifism?

Von Dohnanyi: Pacifism, the power that appeals to one's opponents—appeals to their higher motives and prods their conscience and in so doing succeeds in its goal? Dietrich, I know you know that Hitler and the Nazis have no higher motives, no conscience. They are utterly depraved, immoral—no, amoral. We live in the real world and this regime is like a serpent. We must grab it by its head and break its neck.

ACT 3

Bonhoeffer: Assassination—to kill Hitler—is that what you are suggesting?

Von Dohnanyi: Succinctly put, yes.

Bonhoeffer: But then don't we enter into the same violence as they?

Von Dohnanyi: Dietrich, you speak in absolutes, in ideals. There is no room left for ideals in this present state, only for options that are preferable to others. Only for action that can save us all from catastrophe and the greater evil.

SCENE 2

An ecumenical conference in Sweden, 30 May–2 June 1942.

Bell: From out of darkness a light shines. Dietrich, how are you?

Bonhoeffer: Thank you, George, but pray please that courage may prevail in such an unworthy servant.

Bell: You are too hard on yourself, Dietrich. What you bring to us, at great danger to yourself, is of great worth. I just trust that what you are given to take back is sufficient to convince the Nazis as to your legitimacy in their eyes.

Bonhoeffer: Thus far all is good, but it is always a thin line I tread.

Bell: Well everything you give us is fed on and hopefully can serve to bring this awful mess more hastily to an end.

Bonhoeffer: For our part we are well advanced in our plans. Our network is strong and grows more extensive every day. We are more determined than ever to rid ourselves and Germany of Hitler. Without the head we are convinced we can still save the body of Germany. We are ready, George, ready to move and we will not fail. We must not fail!

Bell: (Laughing) Who would have thought of it, Dietrich? Two churchmen, and we are speaking of murder, the assassination of a political leader.

Bonhoeffer: (Wry smile) The evil deed for the good purpose.

Bell: Means to an end.

Bonhoeffer: No, never just means to an end. Such justification is far too dangerous, allows too much self-serving latitude. Just the means we have to employ in a less than perfect world. Too often, George, our concern for ethics has removed us from the sphere of responsible action. We are too concerned with remaining 'pure' while we let the world around us descend into hell. Ethics must mean for us immersion into the real world and taking the necessary action in that world. We shall worry about perfection of means when the world of perfection is with us.

Bell: A long way off.

Bonhoeffer: As you know, I have been giving this much thought in the *Ethics* I am writing, but every time I begin to write that book events cause me to reconsider and start again. Perhaps that is as it should be.
    As for our plans, we need support, George. We need to know that the Allies will give support and

Act 3

backing to any government we may be able to put in place. It must be made clear to them that there is a real alternative to the Nazis, that there is some hope, some encouragement, that not all Germans are Nazis, that some redemption can come from within our nation.

Bell: I have spoken to our government, Dietrich, and I of course will continue to press your case, but it is not easy. The only words that apparently have resonance seem to be those of war—total war, the complete defeat of Germany and the Axis powers.

Bonhoeffer: They must understand our alternative. Germany is still very strong. Militarily it will be a long struggle and still a bloody outcome. Millions will die. A clean quick strike by us and all this can be avoided.

Bell: I agree, and I promise I will continue to press your line. I have no desire to see what you describe happen. Even now with the Americans and the Soviet Union, it will still be a long and costly bloody struggle, one that should be avoided if possible.

Bonhoeffer: The military is wavering. When things turn bad more will turn. General Beck assures us that through to the highest ranks discontent is simmering. They know the madness of the Nazis and the futile nature of the war. What an insanity to have opened a second front. They are military men; they know war and they have no desire to lead Germany to an ignominious defeat. Give us space. Give us something to work toward.

Bell: That I could, Dietrich, but you of all people know how strong voices for war can be, especially in these days. I can assure you, however, my representations for your cause will be as strong as I can make them.

Bonhoeffer: Thank you, thank you for all your help. If I may say, I appreciate your openness to such things as we have been discussing, your lack of that piety which stalls action. In these times we need to get our hands dirty, even bloodstained. We must be men of action, action to which we commit ourselves and leave it up to God to accept that action.

SCENE 3

The von Kleist-Retzow residence.

Von Kleist-Retzow: Dietrich, paper. I have found more paper for you.

Bonhoeffer: Thank you. A precious commodity these days. My mind is overloaded with ideas. I must write. These things in which I am involved have stimulated me to so much thinking. Ethics, the question of ethics, is totally possessing me at the moment. I am not sure how my work will be received. It is hardly traditional, maybe not even orthodox as such.

Von Kleist-Retzow: Well, orthodoxy is rigorously enforced these days, but not here. (Laughs.) I am sure my paper will be receptive to your ideas, whatever they may be.
  Maria, come in. You've met my granddaughter, Dietrich?

Bonhoeffer: I have only had the pleasure briefly.

Von Kleist-Retzow: She has come to stay with me. Her father, my dear boy, is serving on the eastern front, along with her brother.

ACT 3

So these ethics: must I wait to read them or am I privileged to be the first to hear of such radical ideas?

Bonhoeffer: Ideas? True, ideas only. I've made several attempts to put the ideas into writing, but then feel some dissatisfaction and must begin again. The ethics I am constructing arise out of action, and as actions carry me forward I am compelled to reflect ever more deeply and reshape ideas. In one sense it is all rather frightening, but in another wonderfully freeing.

You know how we have traditionally built up a whole edifice of ethics worked out in theory, in abstraction, and then absolutized them before applying them to reality. From some supposed place of metaphysical purity we have sought to judge all our actions and intentions. But how does this help us in the real world, where all is not absolute, but provisional? We do not deal in absolutes but rather in a struggle to distinguish the better from the worse.

Von Wedemeyer: So without any real guidance are we left only to look to perfection as being so far removed that it offers no help, or do we merely swim in the tide of things?

Bonhoeffer: (Surprised) Very good. A budding theologian?

Von Wedemeyer: A Sunday school teacher only.

Von Kleist-Retzow: And an avid reader.

Bonhoeffer: Good, we need more of those.

Von Wedemeyer: And you were my teacher in my confirmation classes. Don't you remember? Your methods were hardly the norm even then. (Laughs.)

So what then is it that gives us guidance in the here and now if we have no absolute demand?

Bonhoeffer: In Jesus Christ, the divine absolute immersed into the midst of life, with all that makes it provisional, as a human being. In him is our departure point. Our actions must be in accord with Christ in his reality, which demanded not the absolute ideal but the provisional action, the action for the moment. In him the divine and the secular meet. Our problem is that we have set them as opposites: ultimate reality, a supposed Christian principle, opposed to a secular world with, all its ambiguities, calling for decision making that can only ever be provisionally based, never absolute. We have then left people caught between the two, bound in a field of guilt, a paralysis of inaction, unable to live up to their earth-bound responsibility.

Von Wedemeyer: A guilt then assuaged by quick recourse to cheap grace?

Bonhoeffer: So you have read my *Cost of Discipleship*?'

Von Kleist-Retzow: I told you, an avid reader.

Bonhoeffer: Well, there are some things I wrote in that book that I would change now, though I do not recoil from its thesis. Grace is indeed central but it is never cheap. It costs rather everything; the divine gift, but a costly gift, the gift of God's very own son. Costly grace on which we are entirely reliant in the actions we choose. We can but take actions as best we can and then entrust them to the grace of God. If we are conscious of our neighbour and open to the grace of God, I believe we will act rightly.

ACT 3

Von Kleist-Retzow: I beg your pardon. I am remiss, Dietrich. I haven't offered you any refreshment. Tea?

Bonhoeffer: Thank you, that would be nice.

Von Kleist-Retzow: Then I shall leave you theologians to your discussion.

Von Wedemeyer: Pastor Bonhoeffer, it is true I have read your *Cost of Discipleship*, and I believe it to be a most cogent analysis of the problems of the German church and the call to rediscover what it means to truly follow Jesus Christ, though of course my affirmation of your work hardly counts for much. (Laughs.)

Bonhoeffer: You sell yourself too short, Miss Wedemeyer. I think that you, by the few words that you have said, perfectly understand my work.

By repetitive intonation, almost as a magical incantation, of the words 'grace,' 'grace,' 'it's all grace,' we have emptied our faith of any ethical demand, there is no cost to discipleship. We forget the cost of that grace we so easily invoke to God.

Von Wedemeyer: And the call to discipleship is a demanding call.

Bonhoeffer: True. As I wrote, 'when Christ bids one come and follow, he bids them come and die.'

Von Wedemeyer: 'Unless you pick up your cross and follow me you cannot be my disciple.'

Bonhoeffer: But we have emptied the cross of its meaning and turned it into an innocuous symbol.

Von Wedemeyer: I really enjoyed reading your work. I feel it is far more than a mere intellectual exercise for you. There is a deep giving of yourself in your writing and a call to each of us to give ourselves deeply. I appreciate that, Pastor Bonhoeffer.

Bonhoeffer: Why, thank you. And please call me Dietrich.

Von Wedemeyer: (Nervously laughing) Well, Dietrich, my admiration still stands.

Von Kleist-Retzow: (Carrying a tray) The best that can be done in these times of shortages.

Bonhoeffer: Laughing) If abundance gave us more than this then we would certainly be guilty of the sin of gluttony.

Von Kleist-Retzow: (Laughing) Well, that's one sin the Nazis have saved us from! The only one, but one nevertheless.

Bonhoeffer: And from the East . . . any news?

Von Kleist-Retzow: Disaster. Not even the censor can hide that. The Russian winter. Didn't those Nazis read any history?

Bonhoeffer: (With irony) The 'master race' is not bound by history. So, still alive? There's much to be said for that these days.

Von Wedemeyer: I don't know what I would do if either papa or Max were killed.

Bonhoeffer: Well, pray that you, unlike I, will be spared the loss of a brother in senseless war.

ACT 3

SCENE 4

Waiting for news on the attempt of the assassination of Hitler by Fabian von Schlabrendorff, 21 March 1943.

Beck: Gentlemen, we wait for the news of the brave act that will be Germany's salvation. A toast to that Germany.

All: To Germany.

Voice: Free of Hitler.

Ostler (Looking outside) We are being watched.

Beck: Every precaution we have made; every piece is in place. This time we must not, we cannot fail! Soon we will have our victory. Take your ease while I wait for the call.

(A general discussion breaks out.)

(A group sitting near to Bonhoeffer.)

Conspirator 1: To be totally honest with you, Pastor Bonhoeffer, I have great difficulty with all this. It runs counter to everything I have learned and valued. I think I speak for many of us given what we have been discussing.

Conspirator 2: And you, Pastor, how can one like you—a man of God, of peace—be involved?

Bonhoeffer: As for you, these decisions for me have not been easy. What I have committed myself to runs also contrary to everything that I have learned and valued. You know that it was not that long ago that I was speaking of pacifism. So committed was I to that idea that I was prepared even to go to India and learn from Gandhi. You know Gandhi?

Conspirator 2: : No.

Conspirator 3: : An Indian nationalist leader seeking independence from the British.

Bonhoeffer: But how things have changed. That ideal of pacifism has retreated to just that: an ideal—an ideal which would preclude me from action in the hour when action is needed.

Conspirator 1: : Loyalty and obedience. Vows. Important vows made. Oh, I know we all pledged military allegiance to Adolf Hitler, but the vows go deeper than just to the particular person they are made. If I can't keep one vow how can I be trusted to keep any? A man who can't keep his word but deals in duplicity, how moral is he?

Bonhoeffer: Duplicity even has its place. Telling the truth is not absolute. The philosopher Immanuel Kant gives us the example of a murderer seeking out someone who has taken refuge in your house. He asks, is that person here? To that question Kant says we must tell the truth and turn then the refugee over. This is because for him the truth is an absolute. But how does truth serve the good in such a situation? I profoundly disagree with Kant. There are no absolutes in ethics, but rather the seeking out in each situation the best of imperfect options.

Act 3

Conspirator 3: : I make a pledge to obedience, but obedience to serve the good. When obedience no longer serves the good, I am relieved from it?

Bonhoeffer: No one has the right to demand that you pledge obedience to that which is immoral. That is immoral in itself. In order to avoid that wrong action, an action so contrary to the good, the means by which we are now operating—duplicity and secrecy, even lies—are justified.

Conspirator 2: : So the Abwehr becomes a beacon of morality as we plot the tyrant's downfall! (Nervous laughter)

Conspirator 1: : Here's to moral action, then. (Toasting)

Conspirator 3: You are a remarkable man, Pastor Bonhoeffer.

Bonhoeffer: Just one humbly trying through the mists of ambiguity to do the duty to which God calls him, just as we all are . . . (Phone rings.)

Beck: Quiet please, gentlemen.
(Answering phone) Hello. (Silent pause) Yes, I understand. Thank you.
(To the gathering) We have failed.

Act 4

SCENE 1

The von Kleist-Retzow residence. Knock on door.

Von Wedemeyer: It must be Pastor Bonhoeffer

Von Kleist-Retzow: Please see to it, my dear.

Von Wedemeyer (Opening door) Oh Pastor Bonhoeffer, thank you so much for coming.

Bonhoeffer: On hearing such tragic news, there was only one place I could be. (Takes her hand and stares deeply into her eyes in silence.) And Maria, your grandmother, how is she managing?

Von Wedemeyer: Devastated, totally distraught. She has hardly eaten or slept since she heard the news. (Begins to sob.) Oh, Herr Bonhoeffer, and I . . . I don't know if I am able to cope myself.

Bonhoeffer: Of course, of course, Maria. (Takes her and lightly hugs her.) To lose both your father and brother so quickly. And please, call me Dietrich.

ACT 4

Von Wedemeyer: Dietrich (awkwardly said), thank you, thank you so much for coming, for being here, for being who you are.

Bonhoeffer: It is alright. And thank you, Maria, for being who you are. You have brought light into my life in these dark times. We had better see to your poor grandmother.

(Ruth von Kleist-Retzow enters.)

Von Kleist-Retzow: Oh Dietrich, thank you so much for coming so quickly.

Bonhoeffer: I am only too honoured that you can take some comfort in me in such a time. (Takes her hand.) Maria tells me you have hardly slept or eaten since the news.

Von Kleist-Retzow: I have hardly felt like either. I can still hardly believe it. Oh, when will these terrible days come to an end? Surely none of us can live through too much more.

Bonhoeffer: Hopefully not too much longer. We can only hope events will quickly put an end to this.

Von Kleist-Retzow: So useless, so pointless. The war is lost.

Bonhoeffer: The war must be lost. Christian civilisation, indeed all civilisation, is dependent on this. If Hitler were to triumph . . .

Von Wedemeyer: (Cries loudly.)

Bonhoeffer: Maria, Maria, I am sorry. Your father and brother had no choice but to fight. No one has any choice but to join the army. But I must speak the truth. I am sorry.

Von Kleist-Retzow: It is alright, Dietrich. It is just these terrible events in which we are all caught up, events that seem to carry us along as though we have no control.

Bonhoeffer: I can only offer my support, poor as it is, and pray that God's presence be with you.

Von Kleist-Retzow: But God—where is God in all this? How can we believe in God's presence in all this? I am fearing I can't. Sorry.

Bonhoeffer: No need to apologise. Your questions, even your doubts, are good. They are proper questions and worthy of a response beyond some mere pious platitudes.

Von Wedemeyer: Is there some response then? Some place for God in all this?

Bonhoeffer: To be honest, I struggle with your questions. I do so, for I refuse to fall back on answers that are no longer answers. Where is God in all this? Certainly nowhere where theology has placed him until now.

Von Wedemeyer: Where was God for Jesus as he was dying? Where is God for us when we are dying?

Bonhoeffer: Tortured, tormented on that cross. Is that not where? Is not Christ's cry our cry? God's cry?

Von Kleist-Retzow: And does that cry receive an answer?

ACT 4

Bonhoeffer: The cup, the cup in the garden: 'Take this cup away from me. Must I drink from this cup?' The struggle, the agony finds its resolution then in 'If it be your will then I will drink from this cup.' We are called to obedience, obedience not to those who so easily use the word—Hitler, the Nazis—but obedience to God, that same obedience we find in Jesus—in that obedience to God's will, that obedience which calls us to sacrifice. But this is not the simple facile call made by those like the Nazis, who sit in their comfort and call others to obediently suffer. This is the call of one who in Christ himself exhibits that obedience, sacrificed and broken for the world, given in love. This is where God is present: not in some realm far removed, but in Jesus Christ, broken, pained, in agony, given in love even to death. God hangs upon the cross of this world. Only there do we find God. Only a suffering God can really help us. That God comes to us, walks with us in our pain.

SCENE 2

In the garden of the von Kleist-Retzow estate. Maria Von Wedemeyer reading papers of Bonhoeffer.

Von Wedemeyer: Dietrich, your words are so clear, so beautifully put. They make so much sense.

Bonhoeffer: I am glad you think so, Maria. I feel in this work I am exploring so many new directions and I am not sure how well they will be received.

Von Wedemeyer: Well, you only have compliments from grandmother and me.

Bonhoeffer: My ideas are in a state of constant flux. Each time I complete a section I feel the need to go back and rework it in light of those things going on around us, those things in which I am involved. They raise so many questions.

Von Wedemeyer: You must be stressed, Dietrich, under so much pressure.

Bonhoeffer: Decisions and actions one must undertake that one once would never have countenanced have that effect, I'm afraid. Others, however, are doing much more than me and living more at risk.

Von Wedemeyer: Well, if there is any way I can I would be prepared to offer all the support I can.

Bonhoeffer: (Takes her hand.) You have already offered me more support than I think you could know. From being with you all these times I have learned things I so needed to know. In times like this when hatred and darkness seems everywhere, you have brought some comfort, peace, and light to my world. Maria, I want to thank you for that.

Von Wedemeyer: Dietrich, it is the least that I could do.

Bonhoeffer: I feel perhaps that, given my situation and all that prevails in general, it is perhaps unfair to ask you. And despite all your compliments as regards my facility with language (smiles), I do stumble.
    Maria . . . I would like to ask you to be my wife.

Von Wedemeyer: Then I accept, and you must have no reservations because of all with which you are involved.

ACT 4

Bonhoeffer: (Joyfully laughing): Then we are agreed.

SCENE 3

The von Dohnanyi residence.

Von Dohnanyi: Schnapps?

Bonhoeffer: Rudiger, Klaus. (Takes schnapps.) Thank you. And the urgency of your calling me to your office? I am sure it is not for a family reunion.

Von Dohnanyi: Dietrich, things have turned badly. The Reich Security Office is uncovering rather too much. Of course they are revelling in it. As you know, they have never had too much time for the Abwehr. We are picking up information that since the arrest of Schmidhuber . . .

Schleicher: Schmidhuber . . . Who knows what that poor man has been put through.

Von Dohnanyi: Well, let's just say that Himmler and his henchmen don't exclude too many methods of eliciting the information they want. Anyway, as well as the currency irregularities they've found out about the secreting of Jews to Switzerland, and further, our names have been mentioned.

Klaus Bonhoeffer: Dietrich, we must take every care. You must assume you are under constant surveillance and regard anything you write as read and of course regard your telephone as tapped. Every care, Dietrich, every care.

Schleiecher We are all linked in this and each dependent on each other's diligence.

Bonhoeffer: I understand, but I remain, however, absolutely committed to the path to which we have all committed ourselves.

Schleiecher: (Ironic laugh) Well, friend, it would be a bit late to turn back now.

Bonhoeffer: I suppose you are right. Still, I'm not sure how much resistance I could offer to Himmler and his thugs.

Von Dohnanyi: You're not alone in asking that, Dietrich. Let's just all hope for our success to come before theirs.

Bonhoeffer: And plans at present?

Von Dohnanyi: The von Schlabrendorff plans are coming along nicely and we are fairly sure that nothing is suspected.

Bonhoeffer: But can we succeed this time? This man seems to ride the devil's luck. No wonder he is always so prepared to invoke 'providence.'

Von Dohnanyi: I'll leave the theological pondering to you, but I can say our plans have been meticulously made. This is going to be the hour of our success, salvation for Germany. But, every care, every discretion! Everything is riding on this. We can't afford any slip-up.

Bonhoeffer: I hardly dare to invoke religious language—to speak of prayer, providence, belief these days—but at this moment I don't know. Prayer, hope, planning, commitment to each other, belief—belief in what we are doing. Let us hold fast to faith.

Act 4

Von Dohnanyi: Yes, failure will be total catastrophe for ourselves, for Germany, for civilisation. The serpent's head must be amputated. Hitler must this time be killed! Only then can we find some way to negotiate with the Allied powers and begin to build a new Germany.

Bonhoeffer: The Germany we must build must be radically different, a Germany cleansed of so much that has blighted it, has festered deep inside it before emerging at this time in such a terrible way. And the church? The church has been at the heart of the problem. It has totally failed in its calling and responsibility. Far from the church of the Crucified One, it has become the church of the crucifiers.

Schleiecher: Not only the church. We are all compromised. Look at my profession, the law: perverted to the point where it defends illegalities as law, finds the innocent guilty, and lets the criminals go free. Not even the appearance of neutrality is kept in the Reich courts. Politics? Can anyone ever trust again? Dietrich, I really don't know.

Bonhoeffer: For now, friends: fortitude, belief, valour, and discipline.

Klaus Bonhoeffer And absolute care.

Act 5

SCENE 1

The Bonhoeffer household.

Bonhoeffer: (Dials phone.) Christine? Christine? Hans? Who are you? What are you doing there? (Angrily hangs up.)

(Moves to desk and begins tidying and sorting. Tears up some papers, hides others.)

(Leaves, knocks urgently on neighbour's door.)

Bonhoeffer: Ursula, it is Dietrich.

Ursula Schleiecher: Dietrich, come in. Whatever is the problem? You look like a ghost, at the end of your wits.

Bonhoeffer: They have Hans and Christine. I phoned; a man answered. I am sure they have been arrested.

Ursula Schleicher: O my God! Do you suppose they know then? What of Rudiger?

ACT 5

Bonhoeffer: I don't know. They know something, hopefully not everything. Let's hope it's just to do with the Reich Security Office and their desire to take over the Abwehr, and nothing more.

Ursula Schleicher: Pray nothing else ... I'll try Rudiger and then I'll cook up something for you. You'll need a good meal, because I'm pretty sure they'll soon be here also.

Bonhoeffer: Thank you, Ursula. I fear you are right. I've cleared my office, hiding away anything that may incriminate us. Could you also please call Eberhard?

Ursula Schleicher: Pray for strength. (They hug.)

SCENE 2

Loud knocking on door and voice saying 'Open up.'

Paula Bonhoeffer: Karl, Karl, they are here. (They briefly hug and Karl goes to the door.)

Karl Bonhoeffer: Hello. How may I help ...

Officer 1: We are here for Dietrich Bonhoeffer.

Karl Bonhoeffer: Yes. He is my son, but he is not here at the moment.

Officer 1: We have a warrant for his arrest.

Paula Bonhoeffer: Arrest? But he is a pastor!

Officer 2: We have our orders. Where is he?

Karl Bonhoeffer: He is with his sister. I shall take you to him.

Officer 1: (To Officer 2) Stay here. I'll go for Bonhoeffer.

(Officer 1 and Karl Bonhoeffer move off together.)

(Karl Bonhoeffer knocks on the Schleichers' door.)

Karl Bonhoeffer: Ursula, Dietrich, it is your father here.

Ursula Schleicher (Opening door) Father, who . . . ?

Karl Bonhoeffer: Ursula, please have Dietrich come to the door. There are two men here for his arrest.

Officer 1: (Stepping forward into the doorway) Dietrich Bonhoeffer?

Bonhoeffer: Please. Yes, here I am. I am Dietrich Bonhoeffer.

Officer 1: You are to come with us.

Bonhoeffer: There is a problem?

Officer 1: We shall leave it up to Judge Advocate Roeder to uncover the problem. But believe me, the days of the traitorous Abwehr have come to an end. Come on, hurry, the car is waiting.

Bonhoeffer: (To father) Goodbye (Shakes hand.)
　　　　(Mother arrives with the other officer. Hugs mother.) Goodbye. Stay strong. It will be alright. It is just a mix-up. When everything is clarified I'll be back, but don't bother about dinner for me tonight. (Rueful smile)

ACT 5

Officer 2: (Pushing) Come on!

SCENE 3

The office of Manfred Roeder. Bonhoeffer is led in by Corporal Knobloch.

Roeder: Pastor Bonhoeffer, please take a seat.

Bonhoeffer: For what reason am I here? With what am I charged?

Roeder: Please, Pastor, there are just a few matters of clarification with which we have to deal. Once the truth reveals itself—and seeking the truth for a pastor should not be too difficult a thing—then everything, I am sure, will be well.

Bonhoeffer: But what can these things be? I am a loyal member of the Abwehr. I have even travelled . . .

Roeder: The Abwehr. Yes, we know about the Abwehr. And how is it that a pastor finds himself a member of military intelligence? It is hardly, after all, the usual sort of occupation for a pastor.

Bonhoeffer: I was recruited to the Abwehr due to my many links through the ecumenical movement, links through which I could gather intelligence for the Reich.

Roeder: And such recruitment freed you from compulsory military service.

Bonhoeffer: No. My military service is being carried out through the Abwehr.

Roeder: Far preferable than the Russian front, I guess. And the intelligence you have gathered from your numerous overseas journeys: just what was the intelligence, Pastor Bonhoeffer?

Bonhoeffer: I am not at liberty to say. You must appreciate that this information was, and still is, highly confidential, to be reported only to my superiors.

Roeder: And one of those superiors is Hans von Dohnanyi, who I believe (looks at papers) is your brother-in-law. Always handy to have a family with connections, is it not?

Bonhoeffer: He has been working with the Abwehr for many years.

Roeder: And recruited you. When was that, Pastor Bonhoeffer?

Bonhoeffer: In 1939.

Roeder: Personally recruited on the recommendation of your brother-in-law. We have here—look—your letter of acceptance. Strange though, you retain the original in your papers. Still, the Abwehr do manage their affairs in a manner strange to the rest of us, especially when it comes to foreign currency dealings. What do you know of Consul Schmidhuber, Pastor Bonhoeffer?

Bonhoeffer: Only that he was in Prague. He was with the Abwehr, and was arrested.

Roeder: Correct. Foreign currency irregularities. Not the type of thing, I would have thought, with which a pastor would be involved.

ACT 5

Bonhoeffer: I know nothing of this. I never reported to Prague, but to Berlin. And the Abwehr is hardly the type of organisation to pass around information unnecessarily.

Roeder: Of course not. And do you know to what use some of these ill-gotten monies were put?

Bonhoeffer: No.

Roeder: Something else with which your name has been connected: the movement of Jews to Switzerland. Indeed, again family: your sister—twin sister, no less—Sabine married a Jew and they escaped to Switzerland. Fraulein . . . Friedenthal. The name ring a bell, Pastor?

Bonhoeffer: They were working for the Abwehr.

Roeder: Jews working for the Abwehr!

Bonhoeffer: Yes, I too was surprised. Perhaps even more surprised than that the Abwehr would recruit me, one as you know silenced by the Gestapo, prohibited from teaching and preaching. But as was told to me on my recruitment, anyone who can be of any use to military intelligence may be recruited—Communists, Jews, whatever. We put to good work our enemies.

Roeder: Enemies. Yes, I believe that this is what this is all about. Just who is an enemy and who is traitorous to the Reich? That will be enough for today, Pastor.

SCENE 4

Bonhoeffer's cell.

Knobloch: (Opening cell door) Books, paper, cigarettes, coffee, all accompanied by a letter. We are indeed a lucky man in these days.

Bonhoeffer: Perhaps it is well said that luck is in the eye of the beholder.

Knobloch: Someone like you chooses your luck. With others it is different.

Bonhoeffer: How do you mean?

Knobloch: Well why would someone like you end up in here?

Bonhoeffer: I don't know. I really don't know what I am really supposed to have done.

Knobloch: Well, Roeder's no fool. He must be on to smelling something. You need to be careful with him, Pastor. He can be very persistent and then ruthless when he finds what he is looking for.

Bonhoeffer: I have no doubt of that, but I can honestly say he has nothing to find.

Knobloch: So you say. It's not me, though, you have to convince. I'm nothing but the custodian, the power to turn the key on order. We Knoblochs lack the fine family tradition of the Bonhoeffer family.

Bonhoeffer: Well, if you mean having the city commandant as an uncle, it hasn't seemed to have won me any favours.

Knobloch: The general has an interest. Haven't you opened your eyes?: Do you really think that someone of your status

Act 5

and someone of mine are treated no different here? Take a closer look, Pastor Bonhoeffer.

Bonhoeffer: Please, if it is appropriate to call this cell my own, sit down, if I may invite you. (Begins making a coffee.)

Knobloch: (Sitting, laughs nervously.)

Bonhoeffer: Cigarette? (Knobloch waves it away.) I can assure you it is not as easy, as you say, as it looks. Perhaps you are right. Maybe my background doesn't serve me so well here—shielded by privilege, not tempered by struggle. I don't know. (Pushes a note to Knobloch.)

Knobloch: (Reads silently, then audibly.) 'Suicide, not because of consciousness of guilt, but because basically I am already dead, draw a line summing up.' You can't. Surely it's not that bad. Others have it worse, down there.

Bonhoeffer: I am, I fear, not cut out for this. I even question God. Where is God? How does my faith now stand me in good stead? I ponder, I struggle, and I . . .

Knobloch: (Jesting) I am not sure I am qualified to be your confessor.

Bonhoeffer: The choices here are somewhat limited as to confessors. Human presence and understanding, a comforting word—that is enough in a situation like this; far better than pious platitudes.
 Would you like a coffee?

Knobloch: Thank you, Pastor Bonhoeffer.

Bonhoeffer: Dietrich, if you please.

Knobloch: Then Dietrich, it seems very hard for you, I see. I can only tell you that you need to hang on. You have family and a fiancée, more than a lot of men here. And the charges, well, they are not of the most extreme kind.

Bonhoeffer: Thank you. In days such as these and in a place such as this, it is human kindness, our shared humanity, which means so much. You know, I believe it is in our ordinary shared humanity, not in our often silly attempts at piety, that God is really found.

Knobloch: I've never been a religious man. Never needed it much, I guess.

Bonhoeffer: My point: We always seek God in the extreme situations, times when there is a crisis, and then we cry out for God as a last resort. 'God, come help me.' 'God come save us.' Come as some sort of magician and solve everything for us. But I believe God is not found at those edges of life, just in times of crisis when we somehow run out of all options except the religious one. No, God is to be found in the very middle of life, in the ordinary and mundane.

Knobloch: Well, hardly ordinary or mundane, these times!

Bonhoeffer: Yes. And in the suffering... our God doesn't deal with suffering and pain by abolishing it. Just look around here. God is here in the middle of all that is happening, in all this pain and anguish. God takes it to himself and immerses himself in it. Only a God who truly suffers can really help us in our suffering.

Knobloch: (Laughing) Well, not quite what I remember hearing in confirmation class. Still, now with paper and pen you'll have others more qualified than me to read your

ACT 5

ideas. . . . By the way, if you need to slip some of those letters past the censor I am able to help.

Bonhoeffer: Thank you, Corporal. You place yourself at risk for me. In such perhaps the real work of God is found.

Knobloch: Well I am not sure if my means are as good as God's but in these circumstances they will have to do. (Finishes coffee and stands up.) Coffee, getting harder to get. Thank you.

Bonhoeffer: Well, truly it is embarrassing to receive so many of these gifts when others have so little. I am sure we can find some way in which to share these around. These cigarettes, take some. I don't smoke much anyway, and give them to some who need them more than I.
You have been of more help than perhaps you will ever know.

Knobloch: (Leaving cell) And keep your chin up. We need more men like you.

SCENE 5

The office of Manfred Roeder.

Roeder: The Friedenthal affair. You realise, Pastor Bonhoeffer, that you were assisting Jews to escape the Reich at a time when it was expressly forbidden by law to do so? Do you often break the law?

Bonhoeffer: No, it is not my habit to break the law. My attitude to the civil law has been made clear in my writing. The duty of Christian obedience to the authorities, as I understand it, is made clearly in my exposition of Romans 13 in my book *The Cost of Discipleship*. It has seldom, I believe, been expressed more strongly than there.

Roeder: We have examined your work. But Pastor, have you lived up to the ideal you expressed there?

Bonhoeffer: I believe so. As I have said, my previous problems with the Gestapo arose only over the issue of the state intruding into church affairs. I have never questioned the legitimacy and right of the state and its authority in those affairs which are political. Indeed, I have loyally served the state in my past four years of service with the Abwehr.

Roeder: Ah yes, the Abwehr, that organisation which sees itself as being above the laws of the Reich. That organisation which, in direct contradiction to the Reich law, aids Jews to emigrate from the Reich. Why Pastor Bonhoeffer?

Bonhoeffer: Dr. Roeder, please appreciate that I am trying to remember a course of events faithfully and truly, but without papers and records I can only try and do my best. Further, the work of the Abwehr is such that to me, as a novice with no experience in such things, confusion was, and still is, I'm afraid, inevitable.

Roeder: The truth, Pastor, that is all we want. That should not be difficult for someone in your position. Should it not?

Bonhoeffer: I am afraid, while I have every intention of telling the truth, I must confess that I may have inadvertently misled you last time we spoke.

Roeder: Yes?

ACT 5

Bonhoeffer: And I must apologise for this, as it may have complicated your investigation. But as I say, this was entirely unintentional.

Roeder: Go on.

Bonhoeffer: I gave you a date as to a conversation with my brother-in-law, Hans von Dohnanyi, concerning the Friedenthal affair. To your question of when this was, my first reaction was that it was a long time ago. I then uncertainly, wishing to give an answer, mentioned the date of Spring 1942. On reflection, that date seems now to me to be too recent.

Roeder: And what makes you now change your mind?

Bonhoeffer: I remembered a long illness that I had, and it was during that time that Hans came to see me, and it was then that he informed me that the Friedenthal affair was underway. The date of my illness was Autumn 1941. It was therefore at that time also that Dr. Schmidhuber became involved in the affair seeking entry visas for the Friedenthal group from a Mr. Kochlin from the Swiss Evangelical Church Alliance.

Roeder: A convenient change of date. So no longer were you, or the Abwehr, breaking the law.

Bonhoeffer: Dr. Roeder, I can only ask that you see this as a genuine attempt at clarification. If I may, sir, may I ask you a question?

Roeder: (Nods.)

Bonhoeffer: First, please excuse me for my complete lack of orientation in legal matters, but I cannot understand why you would let me persist, for example, in a mistake like that over the date of my discussion with my brother-in-law, which made all my remarks inaccurate and unclear and therefore a help to no one. I thus have found myself in the painful position of having to make corrections afterwards, thus giving the impression that I previously wished to make a false statement, when in actuality my only concern is to tell the truth so that this matter may be cleared up.

Roeder: The truth then is a complicated thing. And here I was naively believing that for someone like you it would be such a simple thing.

Bonhoeffer: My excuse may sound feeble, but you will know better than I from your experience that people's memories function very differently, and that some people need some certain outward prompts to their memory so as to reconstruct a situation accurately.

Roeder: I have found people's memories to be most deficient when they have something to hide. Well, I have something that I have been hiding from you which I shall now reveal: you have a visitor.

Bonhoeffer: Yes?

Roeder: Your fiancée, Maria von Wedemeyer. (To Knobloch) Bring her in.

(Knobloch nods assent and goes and returns with Maria.)

Bonhoeffer: Maria, how are you? It is so good to see you.
(To Roeder) Thank you for this pleasant courtesy.

Act 5

Roeder: We are not the barbarians you know that some make us out to be.

Von Wedemeyer: Dietrich, it is so good to see you. How have they been treating you?

Bonhoeffer (With gentle irony) With nothing but tender care. I couldn't ask for better treatment. It is a fine hotel here. (They hug.)

Von Wedemeyer I've so missed you. We have all missed you—but I especially.

Bonhoeffer: Nights can be long here, and days also. Oh how I have missed you.

Von Wedemeyer: When this is all over . . .

Bonhoeffer: Soon Maria, soon.

Roeder: Ahem!

(Bonhoeffer and Von Wedemeyer cease hugging.)

Roeder: Please be seated. (Nods to Knobloch, who brings a seat for Von Wedemeyer.)

Von Wedemeyer: The wedding arrangements are going well. All of the family are so looking forward to the day.

Bonhoeffer: None more so, of course, than I. It is good to know you are all no doubt meticulously organising everything. I am sure it will be a splendid event, a day to be remembered.

Von Wedemeyer: To the end of our days together. Grandmother is suggesting the reception should be in the garden. It will be so beautiful at that time of year.

Bonhoeffer: True, yes it will be. And we hardly dare to deny her her wishes.

Von Wedemeyer: She is organising a chamber music quartet and I have listed for her all your favourite pieces. I have suggested Bach's Mass in B minor immediately following the service.

Bonhoeffer: You know too much about my musical tastes. And you whet my appetite too much; I don't know how I will ever get through my coming days here.

Von Wedemeyer: Then I will speak no more of it. I so love you and would never want to make if it more difficult for you.

Bonhoeffer: Thank you, Maria. (Whispers) You are so beautiful, such a tender delight.

Roeder: Speak up!

Von Wedemeyer: I have some books for you. I am sure you will find so much in them.

(Roeder rises, nods to Knobloch, who takes the books and brings them to Roeder, who leafs through them.)

Roeder: Miss Von Wedemeyer, everything seems to be in order. I am sure you will understand.

(Knobloch hands the books to von Wedemeyer.)

ACT 5

Bonhoeffer Goethe, Dilthey, Rilke. I see not only my musical tastes are well known to you. Thank you.

Von Wedemeyer: The choices were not all mine. The family has been very involved in carefully selecting the works that should be most enlightening to you in your current situation. Read them carefully and savour them. Rilke in particular I know you will find most enlightening.

Von Wedemeyer: Thank you.

Roeder: I am sure you will also understand that I need now also to terminate your visit. You will understand that I am a busy man with much needing to be done. The Reich has many enemies with whom we must deal.

Von Wedemeyer: Thank you for your kindness in permitting my visit here and allowing me to give my fiancée some reading material.

Knobloch: This way please, Miss Von Wedemeyer.

SCENE 6

Corporal Knobloch leading Maria Von Wedemeyer from the office.

Knobloch: You need to be very careful, especially of Roeder. It was not just out of the goodness of his heart that he invited you here.

Von Wedemeyer: Thank you, Corporal. And thank you for your kindness to my fiancée. Dietrich has written to me of it.

Knobloch: Miss Von Wedemeyer, I have a note from your fiancée—an irregular means of bypassing the censor. (Passes note.) You will understand that I am placing myself at risk in doing this. Of course you will also understand that things at the moment are very difficult for a family such as mine.

Von Wedemeyer: Of course I understand, and rest assured that those things will be looked after. (Slips him money.) But please take care.

Knobloch: We all need to take care in such times as these; keep our heads down and noses clean.

SCENE 7

Bonhoeffer's cell.

Bonhoeffer: Something must be here. (Searches binding and spine of book, leafs pages, stops and looks at one.) Ah here, dots under the letters: s n a h f e s o j g n i h t o n w o n k y e h t. But it makes no sense. What are they trying to tell me? (Sits pondering.)
Ah! Backwards. 'They know nothing. Josef Hans.'

Act 6

SCENE 1

The prison block.

Radio: (In background) There has been a treacherous attempt on our beloved Fuhrer's life today. Providence, however, has determined that the Fuhrer survive and continue to lead the Reich to further glories. Even now, strenuous efforts are being made to find the perpetrators—cowards who had close and direct access to the Fuhrer. These investigations are expected soon to uncover the plot and bring those responsible to justice.

(Knobloch walks to Bonhoeffer's cell.)

Knobloch It's all up now. I suppose you are yet to hear: an attempt on Hitler's life.

Bonhoeffer: (Appearing disinterested) Successful?

Knobloch: No. The mad man won't go down till he takes all of Germany with him.

Bonhoeffer: True, I'm afraid. I guess we can only all wait now for the worst. Hitler will be in a rage and his vengeance will have no bounds.

Knobloch: So you will wait? Wait? If we wait here we are all dead. Make a run for it. I have no ambition to be martyred for 'the glorious Fuhrer.' (Mockingly makes Nazi salute.)

Bonhoeffer: It could be done?

Knobloch: Of course. Do you seriously want to escape, or do you want to wait for Hitler's men? The Gestapo will uncover this in days. A case placed under the table by one of Hitler's confidants. It's going to unravel quickly, this conspiracy. If you are involved move quickly; you haven't got much time.

Bonhoeffer: And you? Why do you want to run for it?

Knobloch: This is a hellhole here and it won't get better. The Americans and British will reduce Berlin to rubble. I've no desire to be under that rubble trapped in a hellhole prison like this.

Bonhoeffer: You are serious then. You will need to liaise with my family. They can make all the arrangements for us both. They still have connections that will help and I will vouch for you. . . . And now the pastor is seeking to escape from lawful custody. (They both laugh.) Thank you, thank you. We are each doing our little part.

ACT 6

SCENE 2

In the Wehrmacht in Italy, 21 July 1944

Bethge: (Reading Bonhoeffer's letter)

Dear Eberhard,

All I wanted to do today is send you a short greeting. I expect you are often with us here in your thoughts and are always glad of any sign of life, even if the theological discussion stops for a moment. These theological thoughts are, in fact, always occupying my mind but there are times when I am just content to live the life of faith without worrying about its problems.

During the past year I have come to know and understand more and more the profound this-worldliness of Christianity. The Christian is not a *homo religious*, but simply human, as Jesus was a man—in contrast shall we say with John the Baptist. I don't mean the shallow and banal this-worldliness of the enlightened, the busy, the comfortable, or the lascivious, but the profound this-worldliness characterised by discipline and the constant knowledge of death and resurrection.

I remember a conversation I had in America thirteen years ago with a young French pastor. We were asking ourselves quite simply what we wanted to do with our lives. He said he would like to become a saint, and I think it is quite likely that he became one. At the time I was very impressed, but I disagreed with him, and said in effect that I should like to learn to have faith. For a long time I didn't realise the depth of the contrast. I thought I could acquire faith by trying to live a holy life, or something like it. I wrote *The Cost of Discipleship* as though that was the end of that path. Today I can see the dangers of that book, though I still stand by what I wrote.

I discovered later, and I'm still discovering right up to this moment, that it is only by living completely in this world that one learns to have faith. One must completely abandon any attempt to make something of oneself, whether it be a saint, or a converted sinner or a person of the church (a so-called priestly type!), a righteous person or an unrighteous one, a sick person or a healthy one. By this worldliness I mean living unreservedly in life's duties, problems, successes and failures, experiences and perplexities. In so doing we throw ourselves completely into the arms of God, taking seriously not our own sufferings, but those of a God in the world—watching with Christ in Gethsemane. That I think is faith; that is true conversion; and that is how one becomes a human being and a Christian. How can success make us arrogant, or failure lead us astray, when we share in God's sufferings through a life of this kind?

I think you see what I mean, even though I put it so briefly. I'm glad to have been able to learn this, and I know I've been able to do so only along the road that I have travelled. So I am grateful for the past, and the present, and am content with them.

I was delighted to hear from you, and I'm glad you are not finding it too hot. There must be a good many letters from me on the way. Goodbye. Keep well, and don't lose hope that we shall all meet again soon. I will always think of you in faithfulness and gratitude.

Yours, Dietrich

SCENE 3

The office of Manfred Roeder.

Roeder: (Enraged) Lies, lies, lies. Nothing but lies. You have lied continually to me.

Bonhoeffer: (Quizzically) Pardon?

Roeder: Don't play your naive innocent pastor with me. We know everything now—everything, Pastor Bonhoeffer.

ACT 6

Bonhoeffer: I am confused. I . . .

Roeder: Enough! Enough, you Abwehr shit! Hiding, playing your traitorous games, the lot of you. Now you will all hang! The Fuhrer has already ordered the current executions be stopped till we get everything—everything! Von Stauffenberg, your traitorous uncle von Hase, eliminated. But we still have enough mouths to prise open, believe me! Everyone in your circle—Canaris, Ostler, Perls, Sack, your brother Klaus, two brother-in-laws, von Dohnanyi and Schleicher—my goodness aren't we are a traitorous family. We have them all. Swine, or maybe like the Jews they love, swine's not good enough for them! (Leaves abruptly)

Knobloch: The Gestapo found documents in the Abwehr headquarters at Zosen. Totally implicated everyone, including yourself, I'm afraid.

Bonhoeffer: (Weeps.)

(Writes note.) Could you please give this to Maria?

Knobloch: As I thought. You are no clean-skin pastor, heavenly minded, of no earthly use. (Hugs Bonhoeffer.)

SCENE 4

Bonhoeffer's cell. Bonhoeffer finishes writing his poem, then reads.

Bonhoeffer

Self-discipline;

If you set out to seek freedom, you must learn above all things Mastery over sense and soul, for fear that your passions and longing lead you from the path that you must follow. Chaste be your mind and your body, and subject to you and obedient, Serving solely to seek their appointed goal and objective. None learns the secret of freedom save only by way of discipline

Action;

Do and dare what is right, not swayed by fancy, valiantly grasping the occasion, not cravenly doubting. Not in the flight of ideas but only in action is freedom. Trusting in God whose commandment you faithfully follow; Freedom, exultant, will welcome your spirit with joy.

Suffering;

Wondrous transformation! Your hands so strong and active, now bound in helplessness now you see your action ended; you sigh in relief, your cause now to stronger hands committing so now you may rest contented Just for one blissful moment, you could taste the sweetness of freedom, then, that it might be perfected in glory, you handed it to God.

Death;

Come now, greatest feast on the road to eternal freedom, Death, cast aside all the chains of burden and demolish the walls of our temporal bodies, the walls of our blinded souls, that we might finally see that which remains here hidden. Freedom, how long we have sought you in discipline, action, and suffering, now dying we behold you revealed in God.

Act 7

SCENE 1

The Bonhoeffer residence. Karl and Paula Bonhoeffer listening to the BBC radio. Music fades.

Announcer: And now we are to hear from the memorial service for the late martyred German Lutheran pastor, Dietrich Bonhoeffer.

(Karl and Paula, shocked, take hold of each other's hands and weep.)

SCENE 2

Narrator: Dietrich Bonhoeffer was taken from his cell in the military prison at Tegel on 8 October 1944 by a Gestapo commando unit and was taken to the basement prison at Prinz-Albrecht Stasse. There he was able to have brief encounters on the way to the shower with such friends and relatives as Hans von Dohnanyi, Fabian von Schlabrendorff, Hans Bohm, Carl Goerdeler and others.

Unlike many who were executed earlier, Bonhoeffer and his circle were spared for further interrogation. He was therefore on 7 February 1945, in the dying days of the war, given a place in a special convoy taking prominent prisoners to the concentration camp at Buchenwald. There he was held in a specially adapted cellar outside the camp with Josef Muller, Herman Punder, General Alexander von Falkenhausen, and Wassili Kokorin, the nephew of the Soviet minister Molotov, along with the English officers Captain S. Payne Best and Hugh Falconer. He shared a cell with General von Rabenau.

On 3 April the group was taken by truck to Regensburg and Schonberg in the Bavarian forest. During Hitler's midday conference on 5 April 1945, the decision was taken to execute all the Zosen group, including Ostler, Canaris, von Dohnanyi, and Dietrich Bonhoeffer. Bonhoeffer, through an oversight, had been placed in the wrong transport and had to be brought back to Flossenburg for his execution.

In the grey dawn of 9 April, Bonhoeffer, Ostler, Canaris, and several others were hung. Hans von Dohnanyi was put to death in Sachsenhausen probably on the same day, while Klaus Bonhoeffer and Rudiger Schleicher were shot by the SS on 23 April. Eberhard Bethge, whose trial was set to take place in May, was set free when Soviet troops reached Berlin.

The fiancée of Dietrich Bonhoeffer, Maria von Wedemeyer, only learned of Dietrich's execution two months after it took place. Eberhard Bethge and Dietrich's parents did not receive word until 27 July 1945, when British radio broadcast a memorial service for Dietrich held in London.

Maria travelled to America in 1948, studying mathematics before working in the computer industry.

Act 7

After contracting cancer she died in 1977 at age fifty-three.

www.ingramcontent.com/pod-product-compliance
Lightning Source LLC
Chambersburg PA
CBHW070509090426
42735CB00012B/2705